Algarve Wildlife

- the natural year -

Clive Viney

Ray Tipper

FIRST
NATURE
www.first-nature.com

First published in the United Kingdom in 2009 by

First Nature
Bwlchgwyn, Rhydlewis, Llandysul SA44 5RE, Wales, UK
www.first-nature.com
email: **enquiries@first-nature.com**

AlgarveWildlife – the natural year   ISBN13: 978-0-9560544-1-8

Greater Flamingos are found on most Algarve wetlands, sometimes in huge numbers, and are sought out by visitors eager to see this enigmatic bird. Specialist tour companies run safaris from most resorts to see flamingos and observe the traditional way of life.

Contents

Acknowledgements

The authors wish to express their sincere thanks to Dr Ricardo Tomé, President of *Sociedade Portuguesa para o Estudo das Aves/ BirdLife Portugal* for his foreword. They also wish to thank Sue Parker and Pat O'Reilly of *First Nature* for their invaluable assistance and guidance and Rob Petley-Jones for additional pictures.

Foreword

The Algarve is known as a hotspot for tourism in Europe, attracting both Portuguese nationals and foreigners from many different countries. Its long coast, with tepid waters and sandy beaches, along with a profusion of golf courses, are a combination preferred by hundreds of thousands who either choose seasonally the Algarve as their main holiday paradise or select it as their resting refuge throughout the year. This intense human pressure, together with a lack of strategy and vision involving land planning, accumulated during decades has led to an uncontrolled growth of tourist development and construction, and to the destruction and disturbance of important natural areas, mainly by the seashore.

What this book shows us is that land use restrictions and nature protective legislation seem to have still come in time to preserve a major part of the natural wealth of the Algarve, historically one of the most important regions of Iberia for wildlife and biodiversity. *Algarve Wildlife – the natural year* is an excellent book for all those who come to the Algarve for the first time and are interested in seeing beyond the walls of the resort or the boundaries of a pleasant beach. It is also recommended for those who already know the region but feel they might be losing a good part of it. They are right: this is the book that will help them to notice and to appreciate the immensity of detail that composes the Algarve nature they seek to know better.

Algarve Wildlife – the natural year is written in simple language, accessible to all readers, without losing the degree of scientific information that will suit botanists, birdwatchers or other nature lovers. It follows an innovative approach, describing the seasonal variation in nature and landscape, this way highlighting the main aspects that should be noticed in each fortnight of the year.

This book is, in résumé, a complete and up-to-date overview of the most relevant nature patrimony in the Algarve. Moreover, it is also a very useful tool that can be used to plan any trip in the Algarve, helping residents and visitors alike to choose the places, habitats and species that they are most likely to enjoy at any season of the year.

Ricardo Tomé
President of SPEA – Sociedade Portuguesa para o Estudo das Aves / BirdLife Portugal

Finding your Way in the Algarve

The locations of towns, nature reserves and other sites mentioned in this book are marked on the map below, a larger version of which is included for convenience facing the inside back cover (page 162); however, to find your way around the Algarve's many minor roads, lanes and tracks you will need a much larger and more detailed map with a scale of 50,000:1 or larger.

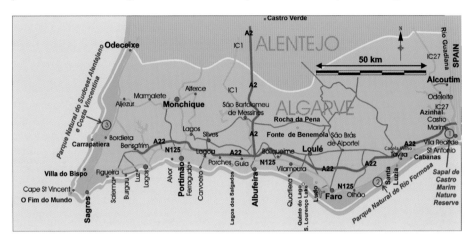

Naming Convention

It is general practice to refer to birds, butterflies, mammals, amphibians and reptiles by their common names, and for this reason we have used the common English names throughout this book. Unfortunately very few fungi and quite a lot of wildflowers do not have common names (or they are so variable from place to place that using them causes more confusion than clarity). We have therefore included the scientific (Latinised) binomial form – *Genus* followed by *species* – when referring to plants and fungi. (It is conventional to use italics when citing species names in their binomial form.) Where a plant or a fungus has a widely accepted English common name we have used it and appended the scientific name. So, for example, you will see simply **Azure-winged Magpie** without its scientific name *Cyanopica cyanus*, but then the plant **Bristle-fruited Silkweed** *Gomphocarpus fruticosus* and the **Parasol Mushroom** *Macrolepiota procera* are referred to in both English (common name) and scientific (Latinised) form.

Where you are likely to hear them mentioned by Algarvian residents, we have also included the Portuguese name for certain of the plants featured in this book. So, for example, you will see one or two references of the form **Aromatic Inula** *Dittrichia viscosa* - **Taveda-de-folhas-revolutas in Portuguese**; however, these are the exceptions rather than the rule.

Abbreviations

Apart from the conventional sp and spp for species (singular and plural respectively) and ssp for subspecies, and the widely accepted km, m, cm and mm for metres, centimetres and millimetres and kg for kilogrammes, we have steered clear of using abbreviations except where they have become names in common usage - for example ISBN for the International Standard Book Numbering system used when referring to other books in our Further Reading section.

Arrival

The Algarve is world famous. It's a place where people come for relaxing holidays on the beach. They eat fresh sardines, drink ice cold vinho verde, play golf on superb courses... and when they retire many come to live here and enjoy all of this in the sunshine amongst the friendliest people in Europe. But the Algarve is even more than that. Between the resorts and into the hills and beyond, the countryside is magnificent and home to an abundance of wildlife.

There are beautiful sand dune systems in many locations along the Algarve Coast.

Most visitors arrive for the first time by plane. From the air the emptiness of middle Portugal is especially obvious as the prairies of the Alentejo make way for the bubbling hills of the Algarve. Through these hills run deep river valleys, many of which are dry in summer, but here and there the sun reflects from bodies of water ranging in size from small cattle ponds to huge reservoirs. Sometimes planes approach down the narrow verdant valley of the Rio Guadiana, the river that separates the Algarve from Spain. Once across the coastal motorway, which seen from the air scores a line between the hills and the greener, more densely populated coastal zone, the blue Atlantic appears. On this eastern approach to Faro the views of the barrier islands of the Ria Formosa are stunning. Seemingly endless empty beaches of white sand enclose blue lagoons dotted with fishing boats.

Approaching from the west the coast presents an attractive blend of rugged sandstone cliffs, beaches and golf courses; the swimming pools of the villas are also clearly visible. As the plane lands amid a maze of narrow channels that work their way through a marshland full of wildlife, very obvious at the edges of this great wetland are the saltpans (called salinas) where Man has harvested salt for thousands of years.

Unpack and unwind but then take time - whether on the beach, the golf course or just pottering about the villa garden - to look at the wildlife that shares your space. Offshore, Gannets might be spectacularly plunge diving for fish, or a small party of Sanderlings could be scampering along the tide line carefully avoiding the waves. On the golf course look out for the extraordinary Hoopoes prodding the fairways, or for waterfowl enjoying the water hazards that the golfers are so anxiously trying to avoid. In the early months of the year the wildflower show is truly spectacular.

Whenever you visit make time to walk and explore the countryside, but do not ignore the historical towns of the Algarve. Peep into the wet markets and look at the abundance of fresh fruit and vegetables and the amazing variety of fish. For those who keep their eyes open there is much more to the Algarve than they could have ever expected.

Access
Ready access to the countryside is usually available to the considerate. There are quiet lanes and unpaved tracks and trails everywhere, and most are open to the public. In Portugal, there is a tradition that anyone can enter unfenced and ungated land on foot - shepherds, goatherds and hunters readily take advantage of this custom. Nevertheless, without permission you should not enter orchards and intensively cultivated land. Hunting preserves and estates can legally prohibit entry, and they are often double-fenced to keep in the game. Take care not to damage the temporary, string-like cattle fences (they are electrified and usually powered by a large battery, sometimes with a small solar panel attached). Saltpan operatives often tolerate casual visitors who walk on tracks, but you must not enter the water or walk on the narrow earth walls (bunds) dividing the pans.

Algarvian country people are friendly. Give passers-by a cheery wave and wish them 'bom dia' (or 'boa tarde' after midday). On private land or in a remote area, indicate to the curious what you are doing and point the direction you intend to go, and you should have no problems.

Just a few words of caution: motorists should take care on minor roads, as drivers of oncoming vehicles never seem to expect other traffic and they frequently cut corners at speed. Also, although the crime rate is low in the Algarve, theft from unattended cars, especially in high summer, is a problem. It is best therefore to take valuables with you and to park where your car can be easily seen.

Hunting

The hunting season extends from mid August to the end of February, but shooting is only allowed on Sundays, Thursdays and public holidays. As ever, there are those who will shoot at anything and at any time, but compared to some Mediterranean countries the situation is reasonably good.

Laws are mostly respected on nature reserves, where the penalties for transgression are particularly severe. Elsewhere, the gangs of heavily armed hunters often seem to have things their way; on no account confront hunters. Persistent bangs in summer are often attributable to automatic bird scarers, which are in use at Faro Airport as well as around many crop fields and orchards. Bear in mind also that fireworks are let off on any excuse, even in broad daylight.

Nuisances

Apart from the need to avoid hunters, the countryside presents few dangers. Occasionally stray dogs around villages can be rather intimidating. Shout to make the owner hear you, and try not to show fear. Threaten with stones rather than a stick – throw the first stone to miss and the dog will be wary of a second.

Mosquitoes and other biting insects can be annoying, but insect repellent should solve that problem. Do not explore hollow trees, however, because hornets often nest there and they can sting viciously.

Scorpions are rarely seen, because they spend most of the time hidden in rock crevices or under logs but a scorpion sting is very painful indeed. If camping, it is a wise precaution to shake shoes before putting them on. Likewise beware of large centipedes – give them a wide berth because they can give you a painful bite.

Although they are seldom seen, an encounter with a scorpion can be a very painful experience.

The Natural Year

Not all years must begin on the first day of January. The Roman year began in March, December being the tenth month. In the Algarve, winter is a growing season and on New Year's Day there are wildflowers aplenty and several species of butterfly occur. It is not until late summer that, because of the dryness and heat, flowering plants become dormant. With the first autumn rain comes the first of the new season of wildflowers. Accordingly, this calendar of the Algarve's natural year begins on the first of August, leaving spring's glorious climax for later.

The year has been divided into 24 half months, and obviously with such short periods there will be overlaps of information. For this reason *the natural year* is best entered at the time appropriate to your visit.

Yellow Sea Aster flowering on the cliffs in April

1st - 14th August - The Peak of the Tourist Season

This is a time when the Algarve's population trebles and the province's infrastructure is tested to the limit. It is a short season but one that is essential to the economy of the Algarve. Tills ring continually and busy beaches echo with the laughter of holidaymakers. Restaurants are full of customers feasting on fat sardines, cataplanas of pork and clams, tuna steaks and delicious almond cakes. The markets abound with luscious fresh fruit, nowadays from every corner of the EU and beyond. Portuguese peaches and nectarines are still in season, as are the superb small green Rainha Cláudia plums. Fresh local figs, both green and black, are at their very best.

Oleander blooms in late summer, long after most of the other flowers have shrivelled and turned brown.

It is hot, often very hot, and the normally crystal air can lose its sparkle so that seascapes become hazy. Inland shade temperatures reach 40°C or even more, but along the coast the lower thirties is the norm and usually a cooling breeze blows off the sea. At night, especially around dawn, it can be chilly and, although rain is unusual, there is occasionally a heavy dew to dampen down the dust.

The land is brown and rivers run dry, but the punctuating trees and shrubs in their various hues remain remarkably green. Nevertheless, forest and grassland fires are a serious risk, and in some years the fires do dreadful damage to the corkwoods and plantations in the hills. Arson cannot always be ruled out, especially in the coastal reserves where greedy developers have their eyes on protected landscapes.

The Rabbit is one of the few mammals to be seen during the day in August.

Away from well-watered golf courses and gardens, plants are resting. Flowers are few, but here and there clumps of pink, white or red Oleander *Nerium oleander* are in bloom, many of the bone-dry thistles still show their colours, and on stony riverbeds both Apple Mint *Mentha suaveolens* and Pennyroyal *Mentha pulegium* are flowering. Due to the slight increase in humidity there are hints of green touching the brown land; the main cause is the new sticky leaves and the few sentinel flowers of the ragwort-like Aromatic Inula *Dittrichia viscosa* - Taveda-de-folhas-revolutas in Portuguese - that lines the roads and covers any uncultivated land.

Everywhere, the large black pods of the Carob or Locust trees *Ceratonia siliqua* - Alfarrobas in Portuguese - are falling and are quickly gathered up and sold to the cooperativas. Most are used as livestock feed or sent to factories that produce locust bean gum, a much used food additive. The pods are the basis of carob chocolate, suitable for diabetics. Incidentally, the large even-sized beans were the original qirat or carat measures used in the jewellery trade.

Carob pods are the basis of carob chocolate, which is high in vitamins but very low in fat.

In gardens, hovering Humming-bird Hawkmoths *Macroglossum stellatarum* stay loyal to flowering bushes, and huge Egyptian Grasshoppers *Anacridium aegyptium* and Praying Mantis *Mantis religiosa* stalk among the foliage and flowerpots.

Few flowers mean few butterflies and so, unlike in temperate Europe, August is a poor month for these insects although a few species are on the wing. Swallowtail, Southern Scarce Swallowtail and Painted Lady are common.

The Egyptian Grasshopper is just as much at home in an Algarve garden as it is in meadows.

In the river valleys of the western Algarve, such as the Bensafrim and the Barão, look out for flowering Bristle-fruited Silkweed *Gomphocarpus fruticosus,* an introduction from South Africa. This member of the Milkweed family, also known as Balloon-weed, is the larval host-plant of the rare Monarch and Plain Tiger butterflies. The first Portuguese colonies of these closely-related species were discovered in 1998 near Lagos.

14

A visit to any of the few remaining river pools will disturb Iberian Water Frogs, Viperine Snakes and Spanish Terrapins basking along the edges, and probably a Kingfisher or a Grey Heron looking for the last of the fish. Grey Wagtails dance among the hot stones, and early migrant Common Sandpipers and Green Sandpipers also appear along these watercourses. Keep an eye open for deep-red crayfish, an introduced species, hiding in the rocky pools with just their long pincers protruding.

Birds are not an immediately obvious feature of the parched countryside, but they are there and can be found most easily during the cooler hours. Spotted and streaked newly fledged juveniles may be tricky to sort out. Although swallows are gathering and bee-eaters are passing overhead, most of our summer visitors remain. Pallid Swifts continue to service nests, some in the trunks of ancient date palms or redundant rainwater spouts. Where there are ripe figs, true to their Portuguese name Papa-figos (fig-eaters) there will be gorging Golden Orioles, the plainer green juveniles outnumbering the adults. Few birds sing during these hot days but at dusk listen for Little Owls and Stone-curlews. This is also the last chance to find Red-necked Nightjars. If looking for nightjars at dusk, keep an eye open also for the large, slow-flying Serotine Bats that appear shortly after sunset. Any tiny fast-flying bats you see will be pipistrelles.

It is in the saltpans that migrants are arriving in force. A visit to the Ria Formosa or Castro Marim reserves will reveal a good assortment of wetland birds. The flocks of Avocets, Black-winged Stilts and Black-tailed Godwits are already large, and with them are parties of Greater Flamingos, Spoonbills and Little Egrets. Where the feeding is good, White Storks and Grey Herons are present. In the coastal salt marshes (sapal), Whimbrel, Curlew, Ruff, Common Redshank and Greenshank occur. Shallow water and muddy margins attract shorter-legged waders such as Dunlin, Little Stint, Ringed Plover, Kentish Plover, Sanderling and Turnstone. Among these will be Curlew Sandpipers, true passage migrants that largely confine their appearances to spring and autumn. Along the shores and estuaries, Oystercatchers, Grey Plovers and Bar-tailed Godwits add to the variety of shorebirds. Ducks shelter in the reserves, and with the resident Mallard are the first of the migrant ducks but, in eclipse plumage, most look drab.

Bolstering the Algarve's population of breeding Little Terns are birds already en route to Africa, and with them moulting Black Terns and the first Sandwich Terns of autumn. Look out for migrant Collared Pratincoles that in flight resemble huge martins.

On the farmland at Castro Marim, the flock of Little Bustards is steadily building up and, with a good eye, cryptic-coloured Stone-curlews can be picked-out on the brown hillsides. The public hide at Quinta do Lago overlooking the freshwater lake on the São Lourenço Golf Course is always worth an early morning visit. As well as local specialities such as Purple Gallinule, Great Crested Grebe, Red-crested Pochard and Gadwall, there is a chance of seeing Little Bittern, Purple Heron and even Glossy Ibis.

Around the coast gull numbers are increasing, and offshore good numbers of shearwaters are passing through. Assemblies of the rare but distinctive Audouin's Gull rest on the saltpans at Castro Marim and Santa Luzia, near Tavira. The smaller Black-headed Gulls are back in force but now their heads are no longer dark. (They never were black; they were chocolate.)

15

The freshwater lake at São Lourenço Golf Course, within the Ria Formosa

This is a good time to compare adults of the different races of Lesser Black-backed Gulls; some have truly black backs, whereas others are almost as grey as the resident Yellow-legged Gulls, and neither type seems particularly keen to mix. Taxonomists, ornithologists and birders have debated for years as to just how many large gull species there really are in the world. Until recently the Yellow-legged Gull was considered merely a race of Herring Gull, but now there are moves afoot to divide Lesser Black-backed Gulls.

Despite the heat, it is worthwhile getting up early and stealing away from the swimming pool or beach for a few hours to visit Castro Marim, Ria Formosa, Lagoa dos Salgados or the Alvor Estuary. Wear a hat, use sun block, and take lots of water.

Lesser Black-backed Gull. Some have truly black backs while others are almost as grey as the resident Yellow-legged Gulls.

15th - 31st August - The Hunting Season Commences

Although it rarely rains and it is still just as hot in the sun, the dark hours are cooling and dawn can be a humid affair. Now it is not uncommon for early risers to awaken to a haar rolling in off the sea or mist clinging to the tops of the hills. It all burns off as the sun rises, although such days retain a certain haziness.

Except for a few straggly diehards such as the yellow carline thistles *Carlina* spp, the stemless thistle Atractylis *Atractylis gummifera*, Fennel *Foeniculum vulgare*, Vervain *Verbena officinalis*, the aromatic *Helichrysum italicum*, various mints *Mentha* spp and large grassy tussocks of the knotgrass *Polygonum equisetiforme*, the countryside is almost without wildflowers. This will soon change. Sentinel flowers of Aromatic Inula *Dittrichia viscosa* and Sea Squill *Urginea maritima* are beginning to appear, and along the margins of tidal rivers look out for Golden Samphire *Inula crithmoides*. On hillsides the shrubby covering of new sticky leaves is from the aptly named Gum Cistus *Cistus ladanifer* - Lábdano in Portuguese. No doubt due to the dearth of flowers, there are few butterflies on the wing at this time of year.

Aromatic Inula

When walking in the hills, nobody will mind if you sample a fig or two from the stunted trees on the dry stony slopes - the black figs are delicious. On the fruit counters in the markets good local table grapes are available. Wine snobs counsel that it's best to consume Algarvian grapes this way rather than in a bottle or two of the usually indifferent but potent local wine. The reds are quaffable but the flinty whites are an acquired taste.

A bonus for anybody walking the hot stony trails in the hills is the chance of finding a basking snake or seeing the Algarve's largest lizard, the strikingly green Eyed Lizard. Although one or two snakes are technically venomous, to be bitten it would first be necessary to catch one (very difficult) and then insert a finger into its mouth! The striped lizard with a long tail seen in gardens is the Algerian Sand Lizard.

Now is the time to get out and see the Woodchat Shrike before this summer visitor departs.

The 15th of August is a public holiday, Dia da Assuncão da Virgem Santa Maria. On this day the summer quiet of the countryside is shattered by the blasts of shotguns - a sharp reminder that the year is moving on. This is the soft start to the hunting season, as from this day it is permissible to shoot migratory birds, which means Turtle Doves, Wood Pigeons and wild duck.

On the ridges and passes camouflaged marksmen jostle for position to blast any doves unfortunate enough to pass by, while in the unprotected marshes and on the cattle ponds hunters seek out resting wildfowl. The countryside bordering the towns is where the fusillades are loudest. Three weeks later, permission is extended to include quails, and on 5th October the season is fully open.

It is not only on land that wildlife is pursued, for this is also the game-fishing season. A visit to the fish market, especially after the weekend, could provide the opportunity to examine impressive White Marlins *Tetrapterus albidus*, Blue Marlins *Makaira nigricans* and sometimes a Blue Shark *Prionace glauca* or even an extraordinary Hammerhead Shark *Sphyrna* sp. Exactly what is caught varies from year to year and much is dependent on the sea temperature: warm seas are best.

This is the last real chance to get out and see the more exotic summer visitors because by the month's end the breeding population of Golden Orioles, Bee-eaters and Woodchat Shrikes will have left, although migrants will continue to pass through during early September. Melodious Warblers, Subalpine Warblers and Black-eared Wheatears can still be located on their summering grounds. The only animals likely to be encountered are Rabbits, Iberian Hares and Western Hedgehog road-kills, but there is a chance of seeing a Weasel as they seem to be busier in late August.

Western Hedgehog: sadly this shy little creature is seen more frequently as road-kill, but fortunately some Algarve gardens provide wonderful hedgehog refuges.

The last pools in the riverbeds are scoured by thirsty irrigation pumps. Many of the Kingfishers will have left the valleys for the brackish water of the coastal marshes, where they are now easier to see. It is worth looking for Spectacled Warblers on the salt marshes around the estuary of the Rio Guadiana; this scarce and mostly skulking summer visitor is a little more conspicuous prior to journeying south. In the same habitat, Northern Wheatears and Whinchats are passing through and migrants bolster the local populations of Yellow Wagtails and Stonechats. Large parties of migrating White Storks are gathering and can sometimes be counted in hundreds, far outnumbering resident birds. As in early August there is a good variety of wetland birds on these marshes and in the adjoining salinas. Especially notable are the numbers of Greater Flamingos, Black-tailed Godwits, Avocets and Black-winged Stilts.

The first of the migrant songbirds are now here. On good days, wherever there are trees there will be Willow Warblers, Garden Warblers, Pied Flycatchers and Common Redstarts, and in shrubby areas keep an eye open for Whitethroats, a misplaced Reed Warbler or even a rare Western Olivaceous Warbler. Towards the end of this period there is often a strong passage of Black Kites and Montagu's Harriers, both of which are most likely to be seen around Sagres, where you might also see sub-adult Egyptian Vultures. Ospreys are passing through the coastal marshes. Two rare migrants to look out for are Red Kite and Roller.

At this time of year many of the Kingfishers leave the valleys and move to the coastal marshes, where they are usually easier to spot.

Although country birdwatching in August requires a dawn start, a decent river valley and much patience and stealth, some of our less obvious species are a touch easier to locate. Such species include Dartford Warbler, Short-toed Treecreeper, Crested Tit, Blue Tit and Long-tailed Tit. You may also see chiffchaffs, and they are likely to be Iberian Chiffchaffs, but because safe separation in the field depends on hearing the song it is impossible to be certain at this time of year. Azure-winged Magpies and Spotless Starlings are beginning to flock, which makes them more obvious.

At night listen for the repeated call of the Scops Owl - a whistled 'pew' every two or three seconds. This owl is mainly a migrant and can be heard calling in open country and gardens as it passes through. Nightjars, although no longer calling, are attracted to isolated bright lights to feed on flying insects; try to spot them while dining alfresco at your local golf course restaurant.

Red-necked Nightjars are attracted to bright lights in order to feed on flying insects.

As earlier in the month, if time is limited the best places to visit are the wetland reserves at Castro Marim, Ria Formosa and the Alvor Estuary. At Castro Marim, among the gulls passing through will be Slender-billed Gulls and Audouin's Gulls, but do also take a good look at any starling flocks on the fields as these may contain early Common Starlings.

If family demands restrict activities to the seaside, don't despair because apart from the gulls there is a good variety of terns on offer (Caspian Tern, Common Tern, Sandwich Tern, Little Tern and Black Tern). Even from the beach, Gannets can be seen plunge diving, and good numbers of Cory's Shearwaters and Balearic Shearwaters are moving westwards, and occasionally an Arctic Skua flies by, but be careful where you point your binoculars.

Castro Marim, near Vila Real de Santo António, is one of the best bird reserves in the Algarve.

1st - 15th September - Salt and Almonds

The weather remains mostly fine and sunny and on many days the temperature quickly reaches the low thirties, but the nights are cooler and at dawn there can be a definite autumnal nip in the air. At the end of this period there may be times when the skies darken and rain threatens, but in the lowlands it doesn't usually amount to much. The sea and the swimming pools are cooling down and the overseas sun-seekers have mostly stopped arriving, but many Portuguese prefer to take their holidays at this time. Nevertheless, overall visitor numbers are down and in the towns it is already easier to park and restaurateurs are welcoming back their old clientele like long lost friends. A few swifts, swallows and martins linger, but most are departing along with the holidaymakers; although in a different direction.

Around freshwater margins, Purple Loosetrife *Lythrum salicaria* and Great Willowherb *Epilobium hirsutum* remain in bloom and provide a welcome splash of colour. Elsewhere the countryside is still parched, but the waysides are at last bordered with green and gold swathes of Aromatic Inula *Dittrichia viscosa*. Thistles such as Atractylis *Atractylis gummifera* and *Carlina racemosa* are in flower. Here and there the extraordinary flower heads of the Century Plant *Agave americana* tower up to 7m tall. This unusual plant hails from Mexico and its common name is derived from the long time it usually takes to flower there - although in the Algarve it blooms within a mere five or six years. After flowering the plant dies, but invariably there are others nearby ready to take its place. Country people have long used the sharp points on the end of the very tough leaves as rudimentary needles.

In the hills there are blackberries to pick from the bramble bushes *Rubus* spp but here the fruit is small and woody and so collecting them is hardly worth the effort. The yellowy-green apple-like fruits in the hedges are Quinces *Cydonia oblonga*. They are unpalatable when raw but are boiled down to make marmelada, a thick paste that is spread on bread and sometimes eaten with cheese; this may be the origin of the word marmalade. Quinces are also cut in half and put across the necks of containers of fermenting wine to act as an indicator. When the fruit ceases to be discoloured, the fermentation process has finished.

Carlina racemosa

Large, reddish brown Pomegranates *Punica granatum* are ripening on the trees. This useful fruit from southwest Asia is mentioned several times in the Bible and for centuries has been used as a fertility symbol. Although best known as fresh fruit, pomegranates are also used to make red dye, a cocktail mixer (grenadine) and a medicine to combat tapeworms.

Two small trees in the pistachio family, the Turpentine Tree *Pistacia terebinthus* and the Mastic Tree *Pistacia lentiscus* are full of small red berries that become darker with age. These berries are a valuable food source for frugivorous birds such as Blackcap and, in early winter, visiting Redwings. Formerly, in the Algarve and elsewhere, resin was extracted from the Mastic Tree and used medicinally as well as to make varnish and even chewing gum.

Avocets are often found where there are salinas (saltpans).

At the beginning of the month, the rattle of canes pervades the countryside as the last of the almonds are knocked off the trees. Almonds are gathered after figs but before olives. Traditionally almonds have played an important role in the Algarve, and not only as an excellent multi-purpose food item: the shell fibre has been used to reinforce tiles, oil is extracted from broken nuts, and the shells are used as fuel. Almond shells were formerly used to fire the kilns that produce Santa Catarina tiles. These kilns are responsible for the alarming but short-lived black clouds that occur around Tavira and São Brás.

New plantings of almonds are rare, and nowadays it is a diminishing crop as the old trees are not properly maintained and so yield less.

For those of us lucky enough to live in the Algarve, the almond has a special place in our hearts, for this is the first tree to bloom in the New Year, signalling that spring has arrived.

In coastal areas of the eastern Algarve, sea salt is harvested commercially by solar evaporation, a process dating back to Roman times. The salt is produced by using the sun's heat to evaporate seawater from large concentrating ponds known as saltpans or, here in Portugal, as salinas. In each pan the salt content of the brine is gradually increased to saturation level. At this point the salt crystals settle out and the liquid (known as bittern) is drained off; then the salt is harvested.

Harvesting begins in early September and continues through the autumn. The larger companies are highly mechanised, but on the smaller salinas teams of workers still armed with traditional implements and small tractors descend upon the snowy pans, so that the normally empty salinas are transformed into a Lowryesque landscape. At the centres of operations, huge mounds of salt appear.

The salinas operators are normally tolerant of visitors but this is not the time to test goodwill, especially by obstructing their narrow roads with vehicles.

The main harvesting time for salt in the Algarve is in September.

Our special summer birds have left but others of the same species might be seen passing through. Although for most birds the breeding season has long finished, Common Waxbills are busier than ever constructing and using their large bottle-shaped nests, which are placed obviously in bushes. This introduced African species is well established in the Algarve and has readily filled an available niche. The twittering flocks of this tiny bird buzz around gardens, reedbeds and cultivated land in a most un-European fashion, appearing more like the flocks of tropical munias that skip across Asian rice paddies.

Now is the time to get to grips with our two migrant flycatchers. They pass through in greater numbers and can quite easily be found hawking flies from trees in large gardens and orchards. The Spotted Flycatcher is the larger of the two and is best distinguished by its streaked breast and its classic flycatching behaviour, sallying forth from an exposed perch. At this time Pied Flycatchers are also brown but are darker and always show a white patch of varying size on the wing. The immaculate black and white males, as shown in field guides, are never seen in this plumage on autumn passage as they have moulted into winter brown. Common Redstarts are also in the trees; they are forever quivering their rusty-red tails.

The Pied Flycatcher is the smaller of the Algarve's two migrant species of flycatchers.

Migrant Willow Warblers and Common Chiffchaffs may turn up anywhere, often with the more distinctive Northern Wheatear, whose name refers to its striking white rump or 'white arse'.

Zitting Cisticola

Tree Pipits and Tawny Pipits are widespread and the various races of Yellow Wagtail in their confusing autumnal dress are also passing through. Migrant Whinchats and Stonechats are often available for direct comparison, but beware of female and juvenile Stonechats which, in this part of the world, often have a pale eyebrow. Zitting Cisticolas are common, but less obvious in the reedbeds are both species of reed warblers.

In the same habitat Cetti's Warblers are betrayed, as ever, by their explosive bursts of song. Migration is as strong as ever in the wetlands and, as in August, a visit to any of the coastal reserves should be handsomely rewarded with an exciting range of species. Black Kites and Montagu's Harriers are still passing through, and if you spot an unusual bird of prey do bear in mind that it could be a juvenile Egyptian Vulture. The numbers of Greater Flamingos, Black-winged Stilts, Avocets and Black-tailed Godwits are even greater now, and there are still plenty of other shorebirds in dull, non-breeding and juvenile plumages to sort out. For the wader connoisseur this is a good time to try to locate a rare Marsh Sandpiper, particularly at Castro Marim. Duck numbers and variety are increasing. Look carefully for eclipse male and female Garganey hidden among the Teal. There are, however, precious few passerines on the marshes in September.

The European Chameleon is more easily found in September, when mating takes place and the females descend from the bushes to the ground to lay their eggs.

A few more butterflies are about. In particular, in the hills where the Strawberry Tree *Arbutus unedo* grows, watch out for the Two-tailed Pasha, a large butterfly that looks as if it could belong to a more tropical environment, but it is truly native. European Chameleons are also a surprise encounter. Although quite numerous in the eastern Algarve they are not often noticed because for most of the year they keep to bushes. In September, however, after some vigorous mating rituals the females descend to ground level to deposit eggs, and they can be seen moving purposefully across paths and roads. When you do come across them, these extraordinary, slow-moving and famously changeable lizards with their ever-swivelling eyes can easily be watched as they catch insects with their amazingly long and sticky tongues. For their part, they do not seem to regard humans with any interest.

A good family day out is a visit to the headquarters of the Parque Natural da Ria Formosa at Quinta de Marim, just east of Olhão. There, an interesting and educational nature trail encompasses woodland, scrub, salinas, seashore and a small freshwater lake. A good range of birds in fair numbers is guaranteed. Other features of interest there include a restored tidal mill, Roman remains, Portuguese water dogs and an information centre.

Parque Natural da Ria Formosa near Cabanas, east of Tavira

16th - 30th September - Autumn Equinox

The autumn equinox usually signals a change in the weather. Hot summer days give way to cool, often cloudy conditions and in some years sudden rainstorms test the soundness of summer-baked roofs. Late holidaymakers groan but gardeners grin from ear to ear as balding lawns shade from brown to green and water bills become sensible again.

Apart from the ubiquitous Aromatic Inula *Dittrichia viscosa* there are still few wildflowers in bloom, but showy spikes of Sea Squill *Urginea maritima* seem to shoot up overnight from barren ground - not just in coastal areas as the name implies but also in any dry, rocky places. For most of the year the tough leathery leaves and the large protruding bulbs of this squill are a startling feature of stony hillsides. Now it is the flower, rising from a shrivelled whorl of dead leaves, that draws attention. This plant is very poisonous, but the dried bulbs have long been used for the treatment of heart disease and even in cough mixtures. The erect, evergreen shrub Mediterranean Mezereon *Daphne gnidium,* which has small, white, sweet-scented flowers, is also widespread and, like Sea Squill, the entire plant is very poisonous.

Carob Trees *Ceratonia siliqua* are in flower, and although the flowers are discreet their scent wafts widely. To some they smell of sweaty socks, but they remind other people of warm toast or even of frying mushrooms.

Sand Stock flowers throughout the year in the Algarve.

At Sagres, although the pinkish-purple Autumn Squill *Scilla autumnalis* is in flower, the yellow flowers of a dwarf form of Aromatic Inula *Dittrichia viscosa* dominate the landscape.

Here the pretty and gregarious restharrow *Ononis natrix* ssp *ramosissima* also covers large areas with little green hummocks that still have a few yellow pea-like flowers finely streaked with red.

On open ground, look out for the pretty yellow mullein *Verbascum sinuatum* and the few other discreet plants, such as Greater Sea-spurrey *Spergularia media* and Sand Stock *Malcolmia littorea* - a member of the Brassicaceae. These latter two plants seem always to be in flower all along the Algarve Coast.

Pink-sorrel, also known as Pink Oxalis, forms beautiful carpets in riverside pastures at this time of year, often interspersed with wild mushrooms.

Huge pumpkins - abóboras in Portuguese - which can exceed twenty kilos can be seen in markets or just sitting in the sun on walls, roofs and terraces. The flesh is baked as a vegetable or used as a thickener in soups, and much is crystallised as a sweetmeat. The fruit of another hedge component, the Prickly Pear cactus *Opuntia ficus-indica*, is now ready, but beware of the glochids, the fine sharp spines that penetrate the lips of the unwary. Be wary also of the social wasps *Vespula* spp that build honeycomb-like paper nests in the paddles of Prickly Pear.

Another culinary item worth seeking is Field Mushroom *Agaricus campestris;* the first crop is just beginning to appear in short grass.

Don't be tempted to try the yellow, tomato-like fruits of Apple of Sodom *Solanum sodomeum* that grow on small prickly bushes, often in coastal habitats; this plant is a nightshade and its fruit is poisonous.

A major ingredient is missing from the Algarvian countryside and that is birds of prey, or raptors as they are also called. It is difficult to understand why. The easy answer is to say that they have all been shot or poisoned, but if so why is this not the case across the Rio Guadiana in Spain or to the north in the

Young fruits of Apple of Sodom look like green tomatoes, but as they ripen they turn yellow and then black rather than red.

Alentejo? European field guides show that anything up to 30 species of diurnal birds of prey occur in the Algarve, but in reality birdwatchers can count themselves lucky if a Common Buzzard or a Common Kestrel is on the day's list; anything else is a bonus. The Vowles in their *Breeding Birds of the Algarve* advised that between 1987 and 1992 no fewer than 16 species of raptor bred in the Algarve, although admittedly some were only just hanging on. It is a sad fact that twenty years later many of these have vanished or are managing to conceal themselves remarkably well. All is not lost, however, as two or three days spent at Sagres and nearby Cabo de São Vicente between mid September and mid October should provide enough migrating birds of prey to satisfy the most demanding birdwatcher. This is the southwest corner of Europe, and apparently because of that migrants are concentrated there before proceeding to North Africa.

The Cabo de São Vicente area is much frequented by Portuguese ornithologists and visiting birdwatchers to observe and record the migration of many bird species, including raptors.

The optimum weather conditions for the largest number of birds are anticyclonic with easterly winds. During this time Portuguese ornithologists with help from visiting birdwatchers often log the progress of the migration from various prominent points on the Sagres Peninsula. The geodesic (triangulation) marker known as Cabranosa on the small pine ridge to the west of Sagres is the centre of operations. This locality provides good views over heathland and grassland stretching away to the prominent lighthouse at Cabo de São Vicente in the west, Ponta de Sagres in the south and Vila do Bispo in the north.

On a good day at the Cape, you will see many Booted Eagles together with a lesser number of Black Kites, Honey Buzzards, Short-toed Eagles, Griffon Vultures, Egyptian Vultures, Marsh Harriers, Montagu's Harriers, Hen Harriers, Sparrowhawks and Hobbies. Other annually occurring species are Red Kite, Bonelli's Eagle, Goshawk, Osprey and Eleonora's Falcon. Common Kestrels, Common Buzzards and Peregrine Falcons will also be present, but these will include resident birds.

31

Rare birds of prey such as Steppe Buzzard (the *vulpinus* race of Common Buzzard), Spanish Imperial Eagle, Golden Eagle, Black Vulture and Lanner Falcon have been seen by a fortunate few. As a bonus, Black Storks are regularly overhead.

If this is not enough, try a spot of seawatching by the lighthouse. Should conditions not be good for raptors, then they may be right for oceanic seabirds to pass close inshore. Also, there will be any number of passerine migrants to sort out, to say nothing of resident specialities like Black Redstart and Blue Rock Thrush. For the connoisseur, there may even be Dotterel on the fields near Vale Santos or a roosting Long-eared Owl in the long hedge leading to Cabranosa.

Spoonbills are found on most wetlands and breed in the Ria Formosa.

The wetland bird show is still running with the performers much as earlier in the month, but Little Egrets, Spoonbills, White Storks and Black-winged Stilts are now more obviously flocking; when conditions are right they are busy feeding for the journey ahead. Numbers of Greater Flamingos, Avocets and Black-tailed Godwits remain high. Check the congregating gulls for something unusual, as Audouin's Gulls, Mediterranean Gulls and Caspian Terns are regulars in autumn. A passing Osprey may pay a visit, and in freshwater areas keep an eye out for Sedge Warblers, Bluethroats and a Water Rail or even a Spotted Crake feeding in the open on a dull day. Swifts have become scarce, but it is worth scanning the migrating swallows and martins for Sand Martins or something even more unusual.

A passing Osprey may pay a visit to the wetlands at this time of year.

During or soon after inclement weather is a good time to visit a point overlooking the sea in the hope of finding a storm-blown rarity. There should always be plunge diving Gannets to admire and inshore migrants such as Cory's Shearwaters and Balearic Shearwaters. Common Terns and Black Terns should also be passing. Where there are sandbars, there may be roosts of Sandwich Terns or Oystercatchers and sometimes the counts are high. If you have a strong stomach and a few like-minded friends, and the wind is blowing from the northwest, this is the time to charter a boat or join a deep sea-fishing trip, especially out of Sagres. With luck you may see pelagic migrants such as Great Shearwater, Sooty Shearwater, Wilson's Storm-petrel and European Storm-petrel, as well as Pomarine Skua, Arctic Skua and Great Skua - and there is always a chance of seeing dolphins or perhaps even a whale.

Great Skuas often rob larger seabirds to secure a meal.

To observe migrating woodland birds well, it is no good thrashing around or expecting to spot them during a social hike. Birds become very shy in the Algarve, and so it is best to visit a woodland edge or a large rural garden and just sit quietly with binoculars to hand. Dress in green or brown and find a discreet spot, perhaps under a shady Cork Oak or a Carob Tree and just wait. Before long, one or two autumn migrants will arrive. Garden Warblers, Willow Warblers and Pied Flycatchers are bound to appear and maybe a Spotted Flycatcher will call on its rounds. A Whinchat or a Stonechat might perch prominently and a Common Redstart could come visiting, flirting its red tail. If you are lucky, a Western Bonelli's Warbler will show well enough for you to confirm its identification. Other migrants occurring in this sort of locality include Tree Pipit, Robin, Nightingale, Melodious Warbler, Subalpine Warbler and Common Chiffchaff. As a bonus, some of the less obvious residents might appear – for example Wren, Blue Tit, Crested Tit, Long-tailed Tit, Short-toed Treecreeper, Nuthatch, Jay and Lesser Spotted Woodpecker. With this form of birdwatching birds often come in a rush, but there will also be plenty of time for reflection and daydreaming.

At this time of year be aware that a busy migration is in progress. Keep your binoculars handy and take them with you wherever you go.

Even on the arid stubble fields migrants are stopping. Look for parties of Greater Short-toed Larks, Northern Wheatears, Yellow Wagtails, Tawny Pipits and Corn Buntings.

As ever, mammals are scarce, but the partly diurnal Egyptian Mongoose seems less shy in autumn; sometimes family parties occur with adults, half-grown young and juveniles. Where they are protected, Iberian Hares are often seen.

Look out for the Greater Short-toed Lark in fields once the harvesting activity is over.

Dragonflies are little studied in the Algarve – Red-veined Darter is one of the commonest.

Around rocky river pools look for basking or copulating terrapins. Move cautiously, as they slip into the water at the slightest noise. Most are Spanish Terrapins but the European Pond Terrapin also occurs.

Larger butterflies still on the wing include both of the swallowtails, Cleopatra, and the exotic Two-tailed Pasha, which is attracted to trees with fermenting figs. Around Sagres, you might see a late-flying Cardinal.

When you are out for a walk in the early morning or evening, especially after rain, flies can be a nuisance. Worst of all are the huge horseflies *Tabanus* spp. The males feed on nectar but the females are voracious bloodsuckers and inflict painful bites. They fly with absolute silence, unlike mosquitoes, select a suitable exposed area of skin, and sink their blade-like mouthparts into the flesh - the first indication that they are there. Be warned and take precautions.

Now is a good time to spend a day or two at Sagres to enjoy the spectacle of the autumn bird migration. If you would like to stay there overnight, the plentiful accommodation ranges from an elegant pousada to simple residencias.

1st - 15th October – The Peak of the Autumn Migration

This is an excellent time to visit the Algarve. Although it cannot be guaranteed, the weather is likely to be fine and sunny. Sudden squally showers do occur but as often as not they soon give way to dazzling autumn sunshine. The early morning is usually crisp and invigorating and as the sun strengthens off come the sweaters as a splendidly fine and clear day unfolds. Very occasionally, chill winds off the sea cause coastal fog but invariably this has burnt off by midday. The sunsets are spectacular.

Large yellowy patches of Aromatic Inula *Dittrichia viscosa* continue to colour the landscape and here and there are spikes of Sea Squill *Urginea maritima,* the autumn flowering buttercup *Ranunculus bullatus* and small bushes of white-flowering Mediterranean Mezereon *Daphne gnidium.* On coastal heathland and in the hills, purple patches of Heather *Calluna vulgaris* are appearing.

Sea Squill

The range of wildflowers is limited, however. Look carefully for the pinkish-purple stars of Autumn Squill *Scilla autumnalis* and in the hills the delicate Autumn Snowflake *Leucojum autumnale* and the beautiful Autumn Crocus or Meadow Saffron *Colchicum autumnale.*

Strawberry Tree with fruits and flowers at the same time

Many trees and shrubs are in fruit, including the Strawberry Tree *Arbutus unedo,* the Almond-leaved Pear *Pyrus amygdaliformis* with its hard crab apple-like fruits, Common (Tarentine) Myrtle *Myrtus communis* and the Cork Oaks and Holm Oaks *Quercus suber* and *Quercus ilex* with their fat acorns. An important (for birds) berry plant now in flower is the woody climber Common Smilax *Smilax aspera,* a member of the Catbrier family.

Try the delicious persimmons, or kaki fruit as they are called in Portugal, but do make sure they are almost squelchy ripe otherwise the taste is startlingly astringent. The first of the local orange crop should also be on sale now, but the juice can sometimes be a touch too acidic this early.

On 5th October, a public holiday celebrates the Implantação da Republica and is the opening of the 'big game' season. This is the real thing as Rabbits, Iberian Hares and, in remoter areas, Wild Boar are now on the hunting menu. Sadly, in the extreme southwest migratory birds of prey all too often provide illegal targets that some bored cowboys find too tempting to resist. Well before dawn hunting dogs that have just as eagerly awaited this day flush rabbits and partridges for their masters, and organised parties of fiercely-armed men set off from rural towns such as Martim Longo in pursuit of the pig. By midday, things have quietened down and the rural tascas are filling up with os caçadores boasting of their bags or perhaps telling of the ones that got away. After an afternoon of manly eating and drinking, one or two of the empty-handed may venture forth once again to kill just *something* to show at home. And so it will continue on every Sunday, Thursday and public holiday until the end of February. Let it be said, though, that whilst prey may not always be accurately identified, close seasons and non-hunting days are by and large observed and wetland reserves are respected.

A good country walk that includes a mix of habitat should provide plenty of interesting birdwatching, but for obvious reasons avoid hunting days. Large charms of tinkling Goldfinches are delightful and you will soon pick out smaller flocks of other finches. The passage of flycatchers and redstarts is still strong, and among the warblers will be the first wintering chiffchaffs - often browner than the Willow Warblers, they usually have black legs. Study carefully any warblers that you see because at this time of year Western Bonelli's Warbler, Melodious Warbler, Reed Warbler and Subalpine Warbler and the more easily identified Garden Warbler as well as Whitethroat are still passing through. Robins have arrived and are singing to hold their winter territories - a sure sign that autumn is with us.

In more open country, Whinchats and Stonechats perch prominently and Northern Wheatears are plentiful. If in pastures with cattle or sheep, then look around the hooves and snouts and among the escorting Cattle Egrets and Spotless Starlings for migrant wagtails, which will also be feeding on insects disturbed by the grazing beasts. Here too will be the first flocks of wintering Skylarks and Corn Buntings.

Stonechats often perch prominently on the tops of bushes.

The raptor migration is peaking at Sagres, and so that is the place to be. Even if it's not possible to visit Sagres, this is, nevertheless, the best time to find birds of prey elsewhere but it is a matter of chance. Booted Eagles, Short-toed Eagles, Griffon Vultures, Hen Harriers and Marsh Harriers, Ospreys and Sparrowhawks also pass through on a broad front, and scarce species such as Bonelli's Eagle, Goshawk and Peregrine Falcon are dispersing from their breeding territories. When out and about look to the sky, because apart from raptors there is also a chance of seeing Black Storks as they pass through.

If visiting the Sagres Peninsula, be aware that a selection of Yellow Wagtails, Tree Pipits, Meadow Pipits and Tawny Pipits and possibly Richard's Pipits could be there. You will also see White Wagtails which are not yet elsewhere in any numbers. Around the hilltops look for Crag Martins, but do also check for something special - for example, a transatlantic Chimney Swift. Along the road to Cabo de São Vicente at daybreak, Spotless Starlings line the wires like crotchets on a music score.

Like other pipits, Tawny Pipits are insectivorous birds.

Take time to study these birds quite carefully, because among them there may well be one or two Common Starlings from the north, and in some years perhaps also a Rose-coloured Starling from the east.

And as for black crows, which are scarce east of Portimão, there will be numerous Jackdaws, a fair number of Red-billed Choughs, a few Ravens and perhaps also a Carrion Crow.

Rose-coloured Starling

Undoubtedly one of the Algarve's special birds is the Rufous-tailed Scrub Robin. This much sought after summer visitor is also a little known autumn migrant, moving southwards to its West African wintering grounds. During early October, small parties of these birds can very occasionally be seen travelling through orchards, flittering around and behaving like miniature bee-eaters. Individual birds can sometimes be found moving through bushes behind the shoreline, and while searching this habitat you might also flush out a Quail.

In September the Rufous-tailed Scrub Robin leaves the Algarve and heads off to its wintering grounds in West Africa.

All wetland reserves are excellent bird sites, but in places the harvested salinas will have been drained down for cleaning and maintenance and these will be birdless. The passage of White Storks is peaking, and at Castro Marim over a thousand may be present. Also at Castro Marim, the count of Spoonbills and Greater Flamingos will be high, and flocks of Little Bustards and Stone-curlews can be seen on the farmland. Greater Flamingos seem to be increasing in numbers, and nowadays they range as far west as Lagos.

Castro Marim is a very good place to see Greater Flamingos.

Duck numbers are building up, the principal species being Mallard, Shoveler and Wigeon. At Ludo and São Lourenço Lake, Gadwall, Common Pochard and Tufted Duck can also be added to the list. There is a good spread of shorebirds and they are great fun to stalk and observe, but it's so much easier with a telescope. The numbers of Little Stint are notable, and at the margins of muddy freshwater ponds look carefully for the rare Temminck's Stint. A few Little Terns and Black Terns may linger, and you should also find Sandwich Terns, Common Terns and Caspian Terns.

Common Tern

Some species such as Greenshank, Grey Plover and Bar-tailed Godwit that are not usually seen in flocks are now flocking. Common Snipe have arrived for the winter. Look carefully through the flocks of roosting gulls for Audouin's Gull, which is becoming commoner.

Audouin's Gull

Butterflies are now more plentiful than they have been for several weeks. Easy to pick out are Swallowtail, Southern Scarce Swallowtail, Two-tailed Pasha, Red Admiral, Painted Lady, Wall Brown, Speckled Wood and Meadow Brown. Around Sagres, Monarch and Plain Tiger can be seen at this time of year. Among the whites will be Bath Whites and Clouded Yellows, and most of the blues are either Long-tailed Blue or Lang's Short-tailed Blue. Look carefully at any skippers, field guide in hand, for they are little studied. On stony tracks the Small Copper occurs, and walkers often flush butterfly-like Blue-winged Grasshoppers *Sphingonotus caerulans* that seem to disappear when they hit the ground.

Two small lizards, Algerian Sand Lizard and Iberian Wall Lizard, are active; the first is a ground lizard of open country and the other occurs where there are walls and rocky cuttings. Bright green Mediterranean Tree Frogs clamber among garden vegetation, especially in well-watered shrubberies and even among tomato plants.

It is a time to be out and about, and in the countryside there is much to see and enjoy.

16th - 31st October - Shortening Days

Although usually fine, the latter part of October can be unsettled and in some years the first real rain of the autumn falls. After rain the air becomes brilliantly clear. The nights suddenly feel chilly and alfresco dinners are no longer an option. Before the clocks go back on the last Sunday of the month, the early mornings seem very dark.

Below the surface the land is still bone dry, but despite this there is almost a spring-like feel to the countryside. Obvious wildflowers are still confined to hardy stragglers on cultivated land and the persisting patches of Aromatic Inula *Dittrichia viscosa*. Here and there carpets of fleshy, bright green leaves of Bermuda Buttercup *Oxalis pes-caprae* are appearing, and before the month's end the first flowers of its yellow invasion will be out. After rain, seek out the Algarve's beautiful bouquet of autumn blooms. These include *Narcissus serotinus*, a six-petalled white flower smelling strongly of jasmine; the bright yellow and crocus-like Common Sternbergia *Sternbergia lutea*; Sea Aster *Aster tripolium;* the delicate orchid Autumn Lady's-tresses *Spiranthes spiralis*; and the showy climber Virgin's Bower *Clematis cirrhosa*. Reminders of the parched early autumn still remain, including the huge seed-heads of the late spring-flowering Cardoon Thistle *Cynara cardunculus*, a wild cousin of the Globe Artichoke *Cynara scolymus*.

Cardoon Thistles bloom in late spring, but the seed-heads are still providing food for small birds in October. Cooked properly, the flowers and even the prickly stems are edible.

Autumn Lady's-tresses is the latest wild orchid to flower in the Algarve, blooming in October, some two months later than it does in the UK and Ireland.

The Geranium Bronze is a South African butterfly that was first noted in an Algarve garden in late October 1998. Although regarded as a pest in the Balearic Islands, where it made landfall in Europe in 1990, it seems to do little more than have a penchant for garden geraniums *Pelargonium* spp, which are likewise southern Africa exotics. Large butterflies, such as the swallowtails remain obvious, and on sunny days following a dull spell spectacular male Brimstones and Cleopatras can wake prematurely from hibernation.

Large and showy, the swallowtail butterflies are difficult to miss. In the Algarve, the Swallowtail, seen here, is less plentiful than the Southern Scarce Swallowtail.

The White Wagtail, a very approachable little bird, arrives in late October to spend the winter in the Algarve sunshine.

Robins sing in every garden and gully, and suddenly Blackcaps are common. Freshly-ploughed land attracts larks, pipits, wagtails, wheatears and buntings. By the end of the month, wintering Song Thrushes, White Wagtails, Meadow Pipits and Black Redstarts will have arrived. Less obvious wintering species are Dunnock and Firecrest but they are there to be found. Late October often sees a strong passage of Stonechats and migrating Common Redstarts, and Northern Wheatears are still widespread. Mistle Thrushes are dispersing, migrant Grey Wagtails visit riverbeds, and Southern Grey Shrikes perch on roadside wires. Hilltops and cliff tops are the areas to keep an eye out for Ring Ouzels passing through - southern European birds are of the especially handsome *alpestris* race.

Along freshwater margins, Water Rails show better than usual; study them carefully as a few Spotted Crakes also pass through. In the same areas, Water Pipits are easily overlooked. Spanish Sparrows flock on farmland, sometimes in huge numbers with other sparrows and finches. If winter has come early to northern climes, expect to see flocks of Lapwings and Golden Plovers in open country. This is the most likely time for transatlantic vagrants, so be alert to this if you see any unusual birds.

If winter comes early in northern Europe you can expect to see flocks of Golden Plovers in the Algarve in late October.

Birds of prey continue to pass through, especially at Sagres where Griffon Vulture, Short-toed Eagle, Booted Eagle, Sparrowhawk, Common Buzzard and Hobby can still be expected, with a Black Stork or two as a bonus. Ospreys inspect salinas for easy pickings on their way through.

Griffon Vultures pass over Sagres at this time of year.

45

Two of the most difficult resident birds to identify, especially in fresh autumn plumage, are Crested Lark and Thekla Lark. Both are medium-sized, streaked-brown larks with erect crests. Even the best of the identification literature is confusing, and the 'where to watch birds' guides mostly get it wrong. There is no easy field mark to split them and they certainly sound similar to an untrained ear. The one thing that is sure is that in the cistus-covered hills the lark with an erect crest, which is just about the most obvious bird up there, is a Thekla Lark. Likewise, when visiting the saltpans the lark with a crest is a Crested Lark. As for larks with crests on sand dunes, fields or in the extreme southwest, I suggest they just be enjoyed as larks. For what its worth, Thekla Larks look smaller and greyer but are more rusty-tinged on the tail coverts and are obviously bespectacled, whereas Crested Larks are browner, look larger, behave more sluggishly and in some plumages have diffuse breast streaking. Despite what the guides say, the rust-tinged axillaries (armpits) of Crested Lark are virtually impossible to see in the field. Thekla Larks sometimes perch on bushes, something that Crested Larks don't often do.

If you visit the hills to tick Thekla Lark then look out for Dartford Warblers (which in much of the cistus scrub largely replace Sardinian Warblers) and parties of Crag Martins on the move. Another speciality in these uplands is Blue Rock Thrush, and where there are patches of cultivation there will be parties of Azure-winged Magpies and Spotless Starlings.

Larks with crests seen in the cistus-covered hills are almost certain to be Thekla Larks. Habitat preference is a great help, as they are difficult to distinguish from Crested Larks.

In the protected wetlands wintering duck are arriving, sometimes in huge numbers. The drakes are mostly out of eclipse plumage, making recognition easy. Little Grebes are gathering together on open water and it is worth checking the flocks carefully for Black-necked Grebes. Cormorants are back at their winter roosts. The variety of shorebirds is still good but overall numbers are tailing off. Less common species are still passing through including Bar-tailed Godwit, Knot, Ruff, Spotted Redshank, Curlew Sandpiper and Green Sandpiper. This is the prime time to find Great Skuas and Arctic Skuas offshore, and among the smaller gulls you may find Little Gulls.

Look out for Little Gulls among the other shorebirds.

Take a day off and go for a walk in the Serra de Monchique. Everywhere the Strawberry Tree *Arbutus unedo* is in flower and bearing fruit at the same time. Butterflies now in flight in these hills include Two-tailed Pasha, Red Admiral and the gorgeous Adonis Blue. Around the cottages the air is heady with the scent of flowering Japanese Loquat trees *Eriobotrya japonica,* and along roadsides Sweet Chestnut trees *Castanea sativa* are laden with nuts ready for collecting. Heather *Calluna vulgaris* is in flower in exposed situations, and in woodland another heather, *Erica umbellata,* is also in bloom.

As in the lowlands, up in the hills sentinel flowers of later blooming species are now beginning to appear. Birds are also plentiful in this part of the Algarve, and most days you should have no difficulty spotting such species as the Green Woodpecker, Spotted Flycatcher, Pied Flycatcher, Crested Tit, Blue Tit, Short-toed Treecreeper, Nuthatch, Jay (often feeding on ripe olives), Chaffinch and Serin.

The Serin is one of the many woodland birds to be seen in the Serra de Monchique during the autumn.

1st - 15th November - Autumn Storms

In some years, while the rest of Europe is remembering how to shiver, the Algarve is blessed with a glorious Indian summer (Verão de São Martinho). Traditionally, street vendors sell freshly roasted chestnuts and, during street parties on 11th November held to celebrate the festa do São Martinho, água-pé - diluted, fresh young wine of the year - is drunk. The weather, though, can be moody and swing violently. After a cold start, many days will be brilliantly sunny but others will be windy and even stormy.

Not a buttercup but a relative of Wood-sorrel, and not even from Bermuda but originally from Africa, the Bermuda Buttercup is one of the Algarve's most invasive plants. It is almost impossible to eradicate this weed from golf courses and lawns.

Following the rains more flowers appear, including the invasive Bermuda Buttercup *Oxalis pes-caprae*. The native autumn flowering buttercup *Ranunculus bullatus* is still forming yellow swathes. On much of the arable land, the Portuguese subspecies *lusitanica* of the small yellow marigold *Calendula suffruticosa*, a petite wall rocket *Diplotaxis* sp, and the chamomile *Chamaemelum fuscatum* are in flower. In coastal areas look for the pretty little patch-forming Lesser Sand-spurrey *Spergularia marina*.

Of culinary interest is the extraordinary number of fungi in the woodlands. Some are surprisingly large - Parasol Mushrooms *Macrolepiota procera* can have caps exceeding 30cm in diameter. Several species, including the Parasol Mushroom, which tastes like Wiener Schnitzel, are excellent to eat, but unlike in many other parts of Europe there is no local culture of collecting wild mushrooms for the pot.

Parasol Mushrooms are very good to eat - but like most kinds of wild fungi the secret is in the cooking, and they should never be eaten raw.

49

Even the distinctive and delicious Chanterelle *Cantharellus cibarius*, elsewhere highly prized, is fairly common but remains untouched.

***Cantharellus cibarius*, known in northern Europe as the Summer Chanterelle, is one of the finest edible woodland mushrooms. Distinctive wrinkles underneath the caps help distinguish chanterelles from lookalike gilled species that are inedible.**

Many of the fungi that occur in Algarve fields and woodlands in such great abundance at this time of year are bitter tasting and inedible – for example the many kinds of earthballs and earthstars that in their early stages of development could perhaps be mistaken for edible puffballs.

Some wild fungi are poisonous and a few are *deadly* poisonous; so, before eating any wild mushrooms, you need to be absolutely certain that you have identified them correctly!

Earthstars are fairly easy to find near trees in the Algarve's gravelly fields. Early in their development they look rather like puffballs, but beware: they are poisonous.

The olive crop is usually gathered some two weeks after the first autumn rains. Unlike figs, which are ruined by rain, rain helps swell the olive fruits. Ideally olives are picked by hand, but usually there is such a rush that long canes and poles are used laboriously to knock the fruit onto groundsheets. The olives are then placed into large sacks, and these days most are taken to the cooperativas and exchanged for olive oil.

A lovely old Olive Tree surrounded by Bermuda Buttercups

The rattling of olive canes is not the only sound that pervades the countryside, because this is the time of year when the enthusiasm for hunting reaches fever pitch. On fine Sunday evenings, sometimes in almost total darkness, guns go off everywhere as frustrated hunters use the last of their cartridges on anything that moves.

Butterflies are still plentiful, especially the regular species, and in some years migrant Painted Ladies are everywhere and Monarchs are widespread too. On sunny days along the coast look for the False Mallow Skipper, a North African species with a very restricted European range; in southwest Iberia, it replaces the almost identical Mallow Skipper.

Common Blue (above left) and Monarch (right) butterflies are still plentiful in November.

The autumn migration of passerines has more or less finished although very late Pied Flycatchers, Garden Warblers, Northern Wheatears and perhaps a few Barn Swallows might still be seen. Often there is a large influx of Skylarks and pipits early in the month.

Along the margins of flooded meadows it is always worth keeping an eye out for Water Pipits, and sometimes a direct comparison with the much commoner Meadow Pipit is possible.

White Wagtails and tinkling charms of Goldfinches are suddenly everywhere.

Goldfinch

Huge numbers of duck, notably Wigeon, gather at Quinta do Ludo and Faro Marshes. Lesser numbers occur in other non-hunting zones, such as sewage farms - here politely called water treatment works (ETARs) - Lagoa dos Salgados and on the larger water hazards on the Algarve's numerous golf courses. Occasionally a straying transatlantic species will be among them. On São Lourenço Lake at Quinta do Lago it is possible to see ten or so species of duck in a morning. The Castro Marim core area (Cerro do Bufo) can also be superb.

Wigeon in great numbers winter in the salt marshes and coastal lakes of the Algarve.

Apart from duck, numbers of Little Bustard and Stone-curlew are building up, and in the orchards huge flocks of starlings gorge on ripe olives. Look among the Spotless Starlings for wintering Common Starlings from the north. Despite the names, both species have spots in winter plumage. (Common Starlings have larger spots, and Spotless Starlings are much commoner!) Sometimes parties of Cirl Buntings occur, and this is the most likely time of year for a Glossy Ibis to show up.

As ever on the larger protected wetlands there will be Greater Flamingos, Spoonbills, White Storks and a delightful assortment of shorebirds and other water birds to enjoy.

Although visits to some of the working salinas may be rather disappointing because the water levels are often kept deliberately low, at this time of year there will always be margins that attract birds.

Little Bustard – numbers are increasing at this time of year.

Diurnal birds of prey are still passing through, especially spiralling flocks of Booted Eagles and Griffon Vultures. Scrutinise any vultures, because sometimes a Black Vulture or two travel with the much commoner Griffon Vultures. Occasionally, to the astonishment of the local inhabitants who rarely if ever seem to notice large raptors, a flock of vultures will select an isolated stand of trees and roost there for the night. Rest assured, though, if the next day is a Thursday or a Sunday os caçadores will be taking pot shots at dawn to protect their families from the 'eagles'. For many years a well-known chicken restaurant near São Brás had a dead Griffon Vulture gracing one of its walls.

Griffon Vultures

Little Owl

This is the best time of year to seek out owls. As ever, the eerie shrieks and whistles of Little Owls can be heard at dawn and dusk. Barn Owls remain paired through the winter; these ghostly apparitions are sometimes caught in car headlights, but to see them properly visit the historical parts of towns on moonlit evenings and look along church roofs and castle parapets. In the country, the melancholy but monotonous whistle of Scops Owl and the familiar hoots of Tawny Owls can be heard all through the night. The real prize, though, is the Eagle Owl. In open, often rocky, country its deep muffled 'hoos' carry a very long way and can be heard an hour or so before dawn.

Immediately after a late autumn storm is the ideal time to visit a river mouth or breakwater to look for sheltering oceanic birds. Good sites to try are the mouth of the Rio Guadiana in the east and the Pontal headland at Carrapateira in the west. Leach's Storm-petrels, Pomarine Skuas and parties of Grey Phalaropes are all strong possibilities during or immediately after disturbed Atlantic weather.

16th - 30th November - Autumn Gold

Some late November days begin cold and overcast. Heavy sea mists roll into the river valleys, and occasionally fogbows hang low over adjoining marshes; but, in true Algarvian fashion, the sun burns off the cloud layer and another sparkling day unfolds. Days without any sunshine are uncommon, but at times there are biting winds from the northeast, and in the hills a touch of early frost is not unknown. Be aware, also, that sometimes a storm will transform dry riverbeds into raging torrents the colour of milky tea.

If you are interested in fungi – either as free food from the countryside or simply because of their amzing diversity of colours and forms - now is a really good time to get out into the woodlands of the Algarve. Among the Stone Pines and Cork Oaks you will find many beautiful species including russulas, milk-caps, boletes, corals and parasitic bracket fungi.

Orange-peel Fungus grows on bare earth and prefers compacted soil or clay. Look out for this attractive species on the edges of footpaths through woodland.

If you gather edible mushrooms, such as the Wood Mushrooms pictured above, make quite certain of the identification, because just as in the rest of Europe the superficially similar Death Cap *Amanita phalloides* also occurs here.

Even on the dullest of days in late November, the Algarvian countryside is brightened by a patchwork of yellow hues: fields of vines the colour of well-aged Sauternes, fig trees discarding citrine leaves, and wayside shrubbery ablaze with autumnal old gold. Here and there, rocky outcrops are covered in patches of lovely rusty-gold lichen (right). These are fungi and algae living together in symbiosis, and they add their own splash of colour to the Algarve landscape.

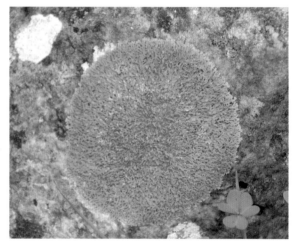

The countryside is surprisingly busy. Everywhere people are collecting olives, not only from their own land but also from waysides and wild (apparently) abandoned land. The poor and often even the elderly lug huge sacks of olives, while those better-equipped use every form of mechanised vehicle imaginable to recover their booty.

The colourful market stalls are piled high with both local and imported fruit.

Oranges are ripening in the citrus orchards, and arable fields are either newly ploughed or covered with winter oats. Much of the market fruit is imported but there are still good Portuguese apples and pears, the rocha pears being good value.

More wildflowers, mostly in various shades of yellow, are coming into bloom but the countryside is still predominantly green. Small yellow marigolds pepper the orchard floors, and on south-facing slopes Bermuda Buttercups *Oxalis pes-caprae* are out.

Prickly Sow-thistle *Sonchus asper* is in flower on wasteland, spikes of gorse *Ulex* sp are in flower in the hills, and on sandy soil look out for the minute yellow toadflax *Linaria ficalhoana*.

In the middle of a sunny day there are still butterflies to be found.

Spikes of golden gorse are in flower in the hills.

Common Chiffchaffs, White Wagtails, Black Redstarts and Robins are widespread. On ploughed fields a variety of larks, Meadow Pipits, Corn Buntings and Hoopoes feed in furrows, while finches and sparrows work their way through the orchards. Pick out the smart cock Spanish Sparrows (they have become much commoner in recent years) and study the finch flocks for wintering Siskins.

Hoopoe

Azure-winged Magpies are rarely seen alone, preferring to forage in flocks.

Occasionally a patrolling Hen Harrier from the north causes panic. Already Corn Buntings are jangling, and along watercourses Cetti's Warblers are singing strongly. In the woods minute Firecrests have arrived, while in open country Azure-winged Magpies move around in large flocks.

Working salinas are often bone dry, but the abandoned impoundments will be full of wintering waders, many in their challenging (from an identification point, that is) drab brown and grey winter hues.

Sort out tubby Knots and elegant Curlew Sandpipers feeding among the numerous Dunlin and, at high tide, roosting Bar-tailed Godwits sleeping among the much more numerous Black-tailed Godwits. Parties of Spotted Redshanks favour this period and can be compared to the much more noisy and flighty Common Redshanks.

In the Algarve Bar-tailed Godwits (above) are less numerous than the Black-tailed Godwit.

Little Tern

In drier areas, Stone-curlews are gathering, sometimes in flocks of a hundred or so. A few late Little Terns are still passing through, and Caspian Terns lose themselves among roosting gulls. The first Greylag Geese arrive at Castro Marim. It is always worth checking the local water treatment works (ETARs), as on the larger 'freshwater' lagoons ducks and gulls will be numerous. Go through them very carefully because, even if there are no rarities, it is a great opportunity to study and learn. At this time, 'uncommon' Common Shelducks arrive and easily identified adult Audouin's Gulls gather on favoured bunds.

Look out for Caspian Terns mixed in with the roosting gulls.

The Little Egret's black bill distinguishes it from Cattle Egret.

A crisp, wintry morning is the best time to visit Ludo. Wrap up well, take a flask of coffee, be at Ludo Gate at dawn and walk to the lake away from the rising sun. The birds and the wonderful light reflecting off the water make an altogether unforgettable sight. Squadron after squadron of ducks, egrets and cormorants pass overhead, but what will linger most in the memory is the evocative whistling of hundreds and hundreds of Wigeon.

1st - 15th December - Interlude

Be prepared for any weather. Some days are sunny and beautifully clear with superb light, whilst others are cold and grey. Early morning mist can just evaporate or turn into persistent drizzle. Always take a waterproof, and have a sweater handy to counter sudden bitter winds.

The seasonal rivers are beginning to flow, but in some years not strongly enough to push away the scars from the summer's gravel extraction or the shaley spoil heaps where pits were scoured for the last of the water. A good flush will see off the Omo packets and plastic detergent bottles - the river is still the favoured place for doing the weekly wash. If you are tempted into the countryside by a turn of spring-like weather, then choose your day carefully: with two public holidays there can be as many as seven hunting days in the first half of December.

In the hills, the Strawberry Trees *Arbutus unedo* are full of bell-like flowers being serviced by many bees, while clusters of tempting red and orange fruit remain. The pulpy, rain-swollen red berries are worth trying, but in truth this is a bland fruit and makes dull eating straight off the tree. The scientific name *unedo* means 'I eat only one', but they do make good jams and jellies and the high pectin content assures rapid setting without additives. The potent Aguardente de Medronho is flavoured with the fruit. The last of the olives are now being gathered.

Friar's Cowl

In sheltered spots, Bermuda Buttercup *Oxalis pes-caprae* is out, and in many places there are still plenty of pretty yellow marigolds. Wood-sorrel *Oxalis acetosella* carpets the woodland floor and large shady gardens. Here and there in the grass, white patches of Annual Daisies *Bellis annua* are out, and on lowland fields there are white carpets of the chamomile *Chamaemelum fuscatum*. On cliff tops, the familiar Sweet Alison *Lobularia maritima* is in flower, and on broken ground look for the similar but much more discreet low matted perennial *Paronychia argentea* and the strapwort *Corrigiola telephiifolia*. In this last habitat, you can expect to see the extraordinary little Friar's Cowl *Arisarum vulgare* with its dark purple hood. Along some rocky watercourses, Bristle-fruited Silkweed *Gomphocarpus fruticosus*, established from southern Africa, is now in flower. Sentinel flowers of various cistuses, thistles, fumitories, borages and even Almond appear. The yellow-flowering creeper *Senecio mikanioides*, another exotic from South Africa, and the extraordinary yellow cones of the succulent Aeonium *Aeonium arboreum* from Morocco brighten many Algarve gardens.

Although many species of mushrooms and toadstools have already disappeared, in woodland it is hard to miss the scarlet-red Fly Agaric *Amanita muscaria*. This is the toadstool of children's books and Christmas cards, but be warned: this magic mushroom is poisonous. It contains muscarine, which can cause nausea, vomiting and possibly coma. Crumbled in milk, it is used to kill flies - hence its name.

Fly Agaric, depicted in so many fairy stories, is hard to miss. This poisonous mushroom, which can only live in association with trees, is most often found on woodland edges.

Red Admiral

Butterflies are now becoming scarcer and are restricted to migrants and commoner species such as Large White, Small White, Clouded Yellow, Small Copper, Wall Brown, Speckled Wood, Painted Lady and Red Admiral.

Paired Clouded Yellows

Wall Brown

63

As ever in the winter months, Common Chiffchaffs, Meadow Pipits and White Wagtails are easy to find, but with the cessation of the autumn passage the diversity of birdlife has reduced. Inland, perhaps because of disturbance by hunters and their dogs, birds are more skittish.

Bath time for a Common Chiffchaff

The familiar Robin

Flocks of feeding finches dominate. Goldfinches, Greenfinches, Linnets and Serins are common, and Chaffinches have come down from the hills and the north in large numbers. With patience, you should also be able to find wintering Siskins. Rare and beautiful Bullfinches occur, and in hard winters Bramblings can be seen too.

In eastern coastal areas, smart male Spanish Sparrows stand out in flocks of finches and sparrows. Azure-winged Magpies form large flocks, as do the much shyer Song Thrushes. Robins, Black Redstarts and Blackcaps are obvious, and Blue Rock Thrushes defend their winter territories. Dartford Warblers are easy to spot on cistus-covered hillsides.

There are not many birds of prey around, but Common Buzzards and Common Kestrels are widespread; the kestrels are often noisy at this time of year. Around Sagres and occasionally elsewhere, Redwings and a few Fieldfares arrive from colder climes, and in recent years one or two wintering Richard's Pipits have caused excitement.

A Grey Wagtail busy at the river's edge

On the wetlands the number of shorebirds has increased and there is plenty of variety. Bar-tailed Godwit, Greenshank and Knot are commoner, and sometimes Dunlin are counted by the thousand. Parties of Lapwings are appearing in damp meadows and along the margins of wetlands. Some Lapwings may come from Central Asia, as exceptionally a vagrant and endangered Sociable Plover has appeared with them. Bluethroats are in the sapal close to the seashore and along the margins of overgrown salinas. Raptors include Marsh Harrier, Hen Harrier, Osprey and Peregrine Falcon. Peregrines cause havoc among the huge numbers of duck. This is the best time to see Caspian Terns; and do look carefully among the Lesser Black-backed Gulls and Yellow-legged Gulls to try and discover a pink-legged and paler-backed Herring Gull from the north. Other visiting gulls at this time include Audouin's Gulls and Slender-billed Gulls, and the Cerro do Bufo area at Castro Marim is a good place to seek them out.

This is an excellent time for a coastal walk to trim down in preparation for the year-end indulgences. If the sun is shining and the wind is not too strong the western cliffs are beckoning. Alternatively, a visit to the dramatic Rocha da Pena, where hunting activities are restricted, could well produce Ring Ouzels, parties of Siskins, Dunnocks and perhaps Alpine Accentors.

16th - 31st December - Winter Equinox

Compared to the United Kingdom and the United States, Christmas is a low-key affair in the Algarve. Christmas cards are still something of a novelty, and Christmas hype doesn't really start much before mid month. Similarly the New Year doesn't seem particularly important, but fireworks are commonplace and in the more remote areas the villagers bang saucepans on the stroke of midnight to chase away any lurking evil spirits and demons.

The pale lemon flowers of Bermuda Buttercup are fully open in the midwinter sunshine.

The variable weather continues. It can be sunny or it can be stormy; it can be beautiful or it can rain heavily. Bitterly cold winds often blow from the north. Residents smile and enjoy the fickleness of the season, but golfers escaping from the frozen north cast anxious eyes at television weather maps. On 18th December 1997, much of the eastern Algarve was hit (literally) by a freak hailstorm of ferocious intensity. Huge hailstones, many the size of golf balls and some lumps of amalgamated stones the size of cricket balls, caused injuries and shattered many car windscreens. For once, vehicles were forced off the notorious N 125, and the land all around turned white. Thunder and lightning, and with it the threat of more devastation, continued all day. During the night of the 22nd & 23rd December 2000, Tavira was struck by what can only be described as a tempest, and the town flooded on the high tide. But the worst Tavira flood in recent years was on 3rd December 1989 when part of the so-called Roman Bridge was swept away as the Rio Gilão rose three metres above the riverside parapet walls.

At midday the now green countryside is carpeted with fully open, lemon yellow, Bermuda Buttercups *Oxalis pes-caprae*. Sentinel flowers of a good number of species, including fumitories, cistuses, periwinkles, borages and several flowers of the Asteraceae family should be showing well. Already Bladder Campion *Silene vulgaris*, Soft Storksbill *Erodium malacoides*, Small-flowered Gorse *Ulex parviflorus*, Rosemary *Rosmarinus officinalis*, the asphodel *Asphodelus ramosus* and the beautiful Paperwhite Narcissus *Narcissus papyraceus* - Mijaburro in Portuguese - are in flower. The marigold *Calendula suffruticosa* is appearing alongside the petite Field

Bladder Campion

Marigold *Calendula arvensis* - Erva Santa Maria in Portuguese - and the first of the long-flowering Crown Daisies *Chrysanthemum coronarium* are appearing. The arum-like Friar's Cowl *Arisarum vulgare* might also be noticed, but usually only by the very observant.

Long-flowering Crown Daisies are suddenly everywhere.

The turn of the calendar year is a great time for fungi in the woodlands around Monchique. These beautiful but inedible mushrooms are *Gymnopilus junonius.*

Black Redstart, a resident and winter visitor

Foraging finch flocks, wintering White Wagtails, Black Redstarts, Robins, Blackcaps, Meadow Pipits, Common Chiffchaffs and, where they are unmolested, Song Thrushes seem to be everywhere.

Look carefully at any flocks of thrushes in open country, because most years a few Redwings and even fewer Fieldfares overwinter, but both species are extremely wary. Dunnocks are good birds to find on hillsides and around cultivated edges.

Painted Ladies can be seen all year.

The Algarve is never without butterflies, and even at this time there are a few to be seen.

The salinas are sometimes drained down, but nevertheless the wetland reserves are well worth visiting as all the usual species will be there somewhere. At Ludo the number of wintering duck has increased even more, but on windy days the ducks often hunker down in the lee of protecting bunds and can be difficult to see clearly. Look for the unusual - perhaps a Great Egret feeding on the numerous grey mullet *Mugil* sp trapped in the salinas ditches; or, if visiting Castro Marim, examine carefully the flooded freshwater margins for a Temminck's Stint or a Water Pipit among the Meadow Pipits. Occasionally, Slender-billed Gulls still flushed pink put in an appearance. By the end of December expect to see the first of the Barn Swallows arrive.

The Paperwhite Narcissus appears in damp places in huge numbers most winters.

Why not walk off the Christmas pudding by following a quiet country lane? There are now more small songbirds (but most not singing) about than at any other time of the year. Many will be finches, chiffchaffs and wagtails although there are plenty of others to find. But the real reward will be to come across a glade filled with Paperwhite Narcissus *Narcissus papyraceus*.

1st - 15th January - New Year

The weather continues to swing from sharply cold to muggy and from overcast to brilliantly sunny. Rain usually comes in the form of showers with the sun not far away. Sometimes rumbling thunderstorms wander around and occasionally a blanket of hailstones briefly turns the countryside snow white. Winds can be bitingly cold and even surprisingly squally. Some mornings, especially inland, are frosty and even icy. Most seasonal holidaymakers return north early in the month, sometimes leaving a legacy of persistent colds and nasty 'flu viruses.

On small remote farms this is the time of the matança, when the family pig is butchered. This is cause for a daylong party when neighbours, local dignitaries and even estrangeiros are invited to eat and drink far too much. Only the men attend the early morning killing ritual, but soon the women are busy in the river washing entrails to make delicious sausages. The best cuts are eaten first, but much is cured and stored away. Nothing is wasted and even the blood is collected and prepared as a black pudding that is usually eaten at lunch that day, followed by a thick stew made with the least productive (and usually the most leathery) of the farmyard fowl. After lunch, the men retreat to the local tasca to drink medronho and aguardente de figos. The feasting continues into the night, the food being washed down with flagons of potent home-made wine and, of course, bottles of port.

Wild Clary adds splendid splashes of purple-blue to the countryside.

Everywhere is emerald green, studded with the yellow blooms of the Bermuda Buttercups *Oxalis pes-caprae*. This pretty introduced flower provides welcome colour to the winter scene, but it is not popular with those who work the land - detested by gardeners because of its persistence and loathed by shepherds because it is harmful to cattle and sheep. (It contains oxalic acid.) Away from its native South Africa, the plant is usually infertile but is readily propagated by the spreading of its small white bulbs - for example by ploughing and weeding. Broad-leaved herbicides have little effect and in the end will do far more damage to the native flora and fauna than will be caused by this attractive oxalis.

An orange grove close to Silves. Here, in November, Field Marigolds battle for the title 'most abundant weed' - one they are destined to lose next month to Bermuda Buttercup.

Great swathes of the chamomile *Chamaemelum fuscatum* colour arable fields white. Patches of orange in orchards are attributable to the Field Marigold *Calendula arvensis*, which is still showing well. Here and there Wild Clary *Salvia verbenaca* adds splashes of purple-blue. The tall blooms of the asphodel *Asphodelus ramosus* attract comment from the most unlikely of botanists. Even more likely to excite is the beautiful Paperwhite Narcissus *Narcissus papyraceus,* which is quite common and in places grows profusely; it is tempting to pick a bunch, but be warned that once indoors its fragrance is intense and overpowering. Some of the Almond trees *Prunus dulcis*, especially the pinker varieties, are already in full bloom. A common belief is that the pinker the blossom the more bitter the almonds.

Even at this early time in the New Year you should be able to see a few species of butterflies including Clouded Yellow, Green-striped White, Red Admiral and Small Copper.

The most widespread wintering bird is the chiffchaff, but whether these birds are Common Chiffchaffs or Iberian Chiffchaffs or both is yet to be resolved. Any small brownish bird, be it in a tree or a bush, sitting or flycatching, will turn out to be a chiffchaff.

Small Copper (male)

Any larger brown bird on the ground is likely to be a Meadow Pipit. Robins are common and Black Redstarts are not hard to find. Large numbers of Song Thrushes also arrive for the winter, but they are exceedingly shy - and with good reason: they are hunted ruthlessly.

Inland, Spotless Starlings, Woodlarks, Skylarks and Corn Buntings move around in flocks, and smaller species such as Long-tailed Tit, Rock Bunting, Blackcap and Dartford Warbler are easier to see than usual.

In cultivated areas, particularly towards the eastern side of the Algarve, Common Waxbills sometimes occur in huge flocks.

In gatherings of feeding sparrows and finches, it is easy to pick out the startlingly yellow male Serins, the dapper male Spanish Sparrows and the shyer Tree Sparrows. Even the very scarce Rock Sparrow can be found in these mixed flocks.

Algarve Song Thrushes have every reason to be shy.

73

As ever, raptors are scarce but Common Buzzards and Common Kestrels occur in fair numbers, and there is also a reasonable chance of finding a wintering Hen Harrier or a Booted Eagle in this southerly corner of Europe.

Although there is a general scarcity of birds of prey in the Algarve, the Common Kestrel fares relatively well, having plenty of nesting sites as well as a good supply of small mammals in the wildflower-rich meadows.

Occasionally on the marshes a Peregrine Falcon puts in an appearance, as they now have an extensive menu to choose from.

The salinas are always worth visiting for a good range of wetland species, but for shorebirds it may be necessary to spend time seeking out areas with just the right level of water. Black-tailed Godwits are sometimes counted by the hundred, and Spotted Redshanks occur in small tight-swimming flocks, often busily feeding. At the margins of salt marshes and along overgrown edges of salinas look out for Bluethroats, and it is here that a spring of Teal might be flushed.

The beautiful Bluethroat is a splendid sight in midwinter.

Most of us make New Year's resolutions, but how many make New Year's lists? Keeping lists of birds or butterflies or even wildflowers seen as the year unfolds can be absorbing and a great stimulus for getting out and about more often. It is interesting and even useful to compare one year with another. Hangover permitting, getting out on New Year's Day and listing what you find is a fun way to start the year. Once the sun is well up, take on a coastal walk that covers a range of habitats.

For example, in the Ria Formosa walk eastwards from Cabanas along the inner shore of the lagoon towards Cacela Velha. As well as the shoreline and adjoining scrubland, the walk passes close to orchards, farmland edges, light woodland and sandstone cliffs; there should be few people about but an abundance of wildlife.

16th - 31st January - Almond Blossom Time

Although it is cold at night - sometimes very cold inland, with sharp frosts - the days are often sunny and the skies remarkably blue. In the early hours of 30th January 2006 snow fell and settled on the hills of the Algarve for the first time since 1954. Obviously, for all but the hardiest souls swimming is entirely out of the question but sunbathing, even in a sheltered spot, can produce a painful red face. This period can provide much needed rain and, unlike the visitors, Algarvians dance for joy when the winter rain finally arrives.

In January the landscape is transformed by the flowering of the Almond trees.

January sees a transformation in the landscape, as bare Almond trees *Prunus dulcis* burst into glorious flower. Some are a beautiful pale pink, others are white, but most are various shades in between. It is simply breathtaking, from the closely planted orchards to the puffs of pink that decorate every hillside. Contrasting with the almond blossom are the carpets of bright yellow Bermuda Buttercups *Oxalis pes-caprae*. Here and there, bare Pomegranate trees *Punica granatum* still hold large maroon fruits, but now they are split and spilling their seeds. Picturesque orchards of citrus trees laden with fruit are everywhere, but many juicy oranges just fall and go to waste. And yet, with the availability of EU grants, in this land so often parched, more and more hectares of these thirsty trees appear.

By the end of the month delicious local strawberries will be on sale in the markets - the first, from nearby Spain, appear around Christmas. One of the joys of living in the Algarve is that strawberries are available until the end of June. The knowledgeable collect wild asparagus spears, and sometimes these are also available in markets. In the east, the collectors are often Spanish from across the Guadiana; they, rather than the Portuguese, seek out this free delicacy.

The first strawberries are usually on sale in the markets of the Algarve by the end of January.

White Broom flowers along the roadsides early in the New Year.

Tracts of White Broom *Lygos monosperma* are in flower in the east. Other obvious hillside shrubs now in bloom or just coming into bloom include the heather-like Portuguese Heath *Erica lusitanica* and Spanish Heath *Erica australis*, Small-flowered Gorse *Ulex parviflorus*, the herbs Rosemary *Rosmarinus officinalis* and thyme *Thymus* sp, and in sheltered parts sentinel cistus flowers herald the dramatic changes soon to come.

77

In the vast hill plantations of the mountainous west, 'mimosa' *Acacia* sp is about to burst forth, and now the stunning beauty of these trees does seem to justify the planting of this exotic.

Acacia trees line the roadside near Bordiera.

Several widespread early flowering species of the daisy family, *Asteraceae,* are out. Perhaps the most readily identifiable of these are the Crown Daisy *Chrysanthemum coronarium* and the more discreet but no less abundant local Field Marigold *Calendula arvensis*. The familiar Annual Daisy *Bellis annua,* Chamomile *Chamaemelum* sp and the dandelion-like Tuberous Hawkbit *Leontodon tuberosus* are common; and in coastal areas look out for the pretty yellow daisy *Anacyclus radiatus*.

Other widespread plants in flower at this time include Ramping Fumitory *Fumaria capreolata,* various sea spurreys *Spergularia* spp, Eruca *Eruca sativa,* Wild Radish *Raphanus raphanistrum,* Black Mustard *Brassica nigra,* green-flowering spurges *Euphorbia* spp, Field Woundwort *Stachys arvensis* and its allies, Common Stork's-bill *Erodium cicutarium* and Musk Stork's-bill *Erodium moschatum.*

Fumitories thrive in the sandy Algarve soil.

You should also be able to find Lesser Celandine *Ranunculus ficaria*, Sweet Violet *Viola odorata*, *Nonea vesicaria*, Milk-vetch *Astragalus lusitanicus*, Intermediate Periwinkle *Vinca difformis*, Purple Viper's Bugloss *Echium plantagineum*, Borage *Borago officinalis*, Fedia *Fedia cornucopiae*, Common Ashpodel *Asphodelus ramosus* and the Paperwhite Narcissus *Narcissus papyraceus* should still be showing well.

In sandy areas the striking purple patches of minute flowers are Sand Stock *Malcolmia littorea*. Look here also for the beautiful but tiny Algarve Toadflax *Linaria algarviana* - one of only five plants entirely restricted to the Algarve - and the petite yellow toadflax *Linaria ficalhoana*, which is endemic to Portugal.

Other gems to seek out are the doll's house-sized daffodil *Narcissus gaditanus*, the larger Hoop Petticoat Daffodil *Narcissus bulbocodium* - Campainha amarela in Portuguese - and the early flowering Sombre Bee Orchid *Ophrys fusca*. Also in bloom are the arum-like Friar's Cowls *Arisarum* spp and superficially similar, but unrelated, birthworts (Aristolochiaceae).

The lovely Algarve Toadflax

Yellow Hoop Petticoat Daffodils

Aristolochia baetica – a birthwort

79

The wetlands are certainly worth visiting, and in wet years there will also be flooded meadows. On damp pastureland look out for birds that prefer this habitat to the saline alternative; such species as Lapwing, Golden Plover, Stone-curlew and even a Quail or a Jack Snipe might be flushed. On the salinas and along the shore there should be a good range of waders and plenty of duck wintering in protected areas. Where ducks concentrate, study them carefully because rarities can turn up and even a North American vagrant is not out of the question. At São Lourenço Lake, in Quinta do Lago, Red-crested Pochards should have returned, and this is one of the few places you can be sure of recording Tufted Duck, Common Pochard and Gadwall.

Stone-curlew

Although Barn Swallows and House Martins occur in early January, it is in the latter part of the month that they begin to return in numbers to their traditional breeding sites. Among the feeding finches, Siskins and Cirl Buntings may be present. With fewer leaves on the trees, small woodland birds are easier to see, and when searching the canopy there is a chance of seeing Goldcrests as well as the commoner Firecrests, as both occur here in winter.

When visiting areas with montane-like cliffs, such as at Cabo de São Vicente or Rocha da Pena, be aware that a few Alpine Accentors winter in the Algarve. During the 1998/99 winter even Snow Finches turned up at the former locality, and the following year there were Snow Buntings.

The cliffs at Rocha da Pena attract wintering Alpine Accentors.

Alpine Accentors breed high up in the mountains, but they can sometimes be seen on montane-like cliffs in the Algarve during the winter.

The almond blossom attracts many bees and other insects. In the middle of a sunny day a good variety of butterflies will be flying and these may include Cleopatras, Red Admirals, Painted Ladies, Speckled Woods and perhaps a Large Tortoiseshell newly emerged from hibernation. This is also a good time to visit O Fim do Mundo – the end of the world. Cabo de São Vicente is the most south-westerly point of Europe, and beyond it the sea seems to go on for ever. The few Algarve-based birdwatchers rarely bother to visit Sagres in midwinter, but they should: in the last week in January 2009 the coastal waters were full of Kittiwakes, a dainty northern gull that is seldom seen so far south. A close look at the gulls in Sagres harbour revealed both Iceland Gulls and Glaucous Gulls, vagrants from the frozen north.

1st - 14th February - Prelude to Spring

The weather is gloriously unpredictable. Within 24 hours the temperature can swing from zero overnight with dawn frosts and icy puddles to daytime highs in the mid twenties. It can even be uncomfortably hot in the noonday sun. Crystal clear nights are brilliantly lit with planets and winter constellations, Orion ruling over all. Sometimes it rains heavily and the seasonal rivers briefly become raging torrents, but sunshine and blue skies mostly follow cloudy mornings.

Yellow Bee Orchid surrounded by spent cartridges discarded by hunters

Unlike in most of Europe, hunting continues through February - but strictly speaking the quarry is restricted to thrushes, and using dogs is not allowed. Spent cartridges littering every hilltop, pass and cattle dam are evidence of hunters' handiwork. It is not so much what is killed, for that is bad enough, but the fear of Man that is imprinted on every bird and animal that survives the frightening winter slaughter.

Trapping as well as shooting take a heavy toll. Traditionally, small birds are trapped and snared by country folk for the pot, seven or eight making a decent meal. Há voadores chalked up on a tasca wall means that small birds are on the menu. Small and delicate spring traps baited with a flying insect are mostly employed; these traps are openly sold in village shops and set around any damp ground. Home freezers soon fill with robins, redstarts and even chiffchaffs. Even today, unfortunately, the practice is as widespread as it ever was, and no doubt this is a factor contributing to the paucity of small birds by winter's end. It is little wonder that birdwatchers are regarded with such curiosity.

Narrow-leaved Lupin

The great variety of spring flowers is yet to burst forth, but look out for purple carpets of the small sand-loving stock *Malcolmia ramosissima* and blue patches of Narrow-leaved Lupin *Lupinus angustifolius*. The Portuguese strain of this particular lupin was domesticated in the 20th century, and it is now grown to feed sheep and cattle in many countries; in Western Australia it is by far the largest grain legume crop.

Blue Houndstongue with its beautifully veined petals

Other flowers coming into bloom include the exotic Golden Wattle *Acacia pycnantha*, Alexanders *Smyrnium olusatrum*, Wild Carrot *Daucus carota,* Honeywort *Cerinthe major,* Blue Houndstongue *Cynoglossum creticum* and the dominant thistles Galactites *Galactites tomentosa* and Slender Thistle *Carduus tenuiflorus.*

The easily identified Borage *Borago officinalis* is now at its very best.

Bold Borage, bluer than the Algarve sky

84

Spikes of the beautiful Field Gladioli *Gladiolus italicus* are beginning to appear on broken ground. In the Monchique hills the first Primroses *Primula vulgaris* will be flowering. Butterflies are also more obvious, and Bath Whites are now flying.

Field Gladiolus on broken ground near Alcoutim

Frogs and toads are becoming active, and it's a good time to find the small and mainly nocturnal Natterjack Toad on the move. Dozy snakes bask on sun-warmed rocks.

Throughout the winter and early spring in the Algarve there are often a few Greylag Geese to be seen at Castro Marim and occasionally further westwards.

Many salinas are drained down for maintenance, making them far less attractive to wildlife. To find wetland birds in any numbers, it is often necessary to resort to the lagoons, the creeks and the shoreline, so an eye to the tide tables is required. Where decent water levels remain there will be plenty of duck and possibly a few Greylag Geese. In most winters salt marshes are flooded and impenetrable, but in other years they may be dry and lifeless.

85

Watch out for the Black-shouldered Kite. This beautiful but unfortunately uncommon species returns to favoured areas very early in the year and is then more visible than at other times.

The relatively small Black-shouldered Kite is sometimes mobbed by other raptors.

In the wetlands, one or two Marsh Harriers should be hunting. Common Buzzards are active, even displaying.

Study any buzzards carefully, for at this time of year there have been several reported sightings of Long-legged Buzzards, a North African breeding species.

White Storks are now back on their nests, and their loud bill clapping is often to be heard - even in the centre of Faro.

Marsh Harrier

Faro from Ilha do Farol

Choose a crisp sunny morning, take a Thermos of hot coffee, and explore a lagoon or an estuary. For lunch why not find a simple restaurant serving caldeirada (fish stew), which at this time of year may include canivetes (razor clams)? Sit in the sunshine and wash it all down with a bottle of ice cold vinho verde. Afterwards, walking back along an Atlantic shore, watch the Sanderlings chase the waves.

Sanderlings skimming over the waves

15th - 29th February - Spring is in the Air

The really cold days have mostly gone, but early mornings can be crisp with a definite smell of spring in the air. It becomes much hotter as the sun climbs, but occasionally fog lingers to midday. Rain is often not far away, but usually it doesn't amount to much more than a heavy shower. In some years, on the other hand, the weather is splendid.

Although the botanical climax is probably still a few weeks off, new flowers are appearing every day. Sadly, the almond blossom has all but finished but the Bermuda Buttercup *Oxalis pes-caprae* continues to provide country colour. A tiny relative of the Bermuda Buttercup, often found growing in flowerpots, is Procumbent Yellow Sorrel *Oxalis corniculata*.

In the hills, Gum Cistus *Cistus ladanifer* is beginning to flower, while Portuguese Heath *Erica lusitanica*, Almond-leaved Pear *Pyrus amygdaliformis* and the evergreen shrub Laurustinus *Viburnum tinus* are already well out.

Gum Cistus, also referred to as Gum Rock-rose, quickly invades tilled land on hill slopes. The leaves are covered in a sticky scented resin.

On waste ground the cress family, Brassicaceae, is showing well, with such dominant species as Wall Rocket *Diplotaxis* sp and Charlock *Sinapis arvensis* - both being yellow, four-petalled crucifers. Roadway verges are full of such flowers as Sun Spurge *Euphorbia helioscopia*, Tree Mallow *Lavatera arborea*, Scrambling Gromwell *Lithodora diffusa*, the striking Large Blue Alkanet *Anchusa azurea,* Purple Phlomis *Phlomis purpurea*, Wild Clary *Salvia verbenaca* and the planted white iris *Iris albicans.*

Large Blue Alkanet

Patches of Purple Viper's Bugloss *Echium plantagineum* and the campion *Silene colorata* turn fallow fields an attractive purple. Look also for the related Bladder Campion *Silene vulgaris* and the Small-flowered Catchfly *Silene gallica* that holds its flowers in a one-sided spike. In these fields you should be able identify the delicate Pale Flax *Linum bienne*, Scarlet Pimpernel *Anagallis arvensis* - which is usually bright blue here - Common Centaury *Centaurium erythraea*, Lesser Snapdragon *Misopates orontium* and Annual Rockrose *Tuberaria guttata.*

The pale flower of a Lesser Snapdragon

Purple Sand-spurrey *Spergularia purpurea* and the sand stock *Malcolmia lacera* colour sandy heaths, while at the back of the beaches the fleshy Sea Rocket *Cakile maritima* is flowering.

In the pinewoods of the coastal eastern Algarve the understorey is dominated by flowering White Broom *Lygos monosperma*. Other obvious wildflowers in these open woods include the yellow cistus-like *Halimium commutatum* and the endemic delicate yellow toadflax *Linaria ficalhoana*.

Sea Rocket thrives on salt-laden sandy shores.

Elsewhere, three species of lupins are blooming and are often found in colourful swathes: Yellow Lupin *Lupinus luteus*, White Lupin *Lupinus albus* and the blue Narrow-leaved Lupin *Lupinus angustifolius*.

A fallow field near Aljezur erupts in a spring blaze of Yellow Lupins.

In wet areas, the unusual Buttonweed or Brass Buttons *Cotula coronopifolia*, an introduction from South Africa, is in flower; and on the ponds so is Water Crowfoot *Ranunculus* sp. Special flowers to look for are the pretty Common Grape Hyacinth *Muscari neglectum*, the parasitic Purple Broomrape *Orobanche purpurea*, the afternoon flowering miniature iris *Gynandriris sisyrinchium* and a real gem *Romulea ramiflora*.

A distinctive butterfly that is fairly easy to see in the hills is the Spanish Festoon (below). Brimstones have now joined their more distinctively coloured cousins the Cleopatras, and other species on the wing include the gorgeous Swallowtail, Red Admirals emerging from hibernation, and the unobtrusive Small Heath.

One of the Algarve's many fascinating broomrapes

Although many of the salinas will be drained down, it is worth seeking out the standing water to find busily-feeding groups of Greater Flamingos, Spoonbills and Black-tailed Godwits. Don't dismiss grebes too quickly, because Black-necked Grebes are often mixed in with the Little Grebes, and at Ludo the Great Crested Grebes will be coming into full plumage. In marshy areas there are more Ruffs than usual, and parties of Teal also congregate there. Among the hirundines there may be migrating Sand Martins. The first of the taxonomically complex Yellow Wagtails should be passing through at the end of the month.

Black-necked Grebes are often to be found among the Little Grebes.

Some Hoopoes remain all winter, but now others are arriving and suddenly these bizarre birds are easier to see. The brownish wintering chiffchaffs are still as common as ever, and in wooded valleys in the hills it is possible to convince yourself that greener looking Iberian Chiffchaffs are present; later they will sing, making identification certain. Barn Swallows are very active making and repairing nests. Nuthatches are calling loudly, and wherever they are present they are fairly easy to see.

Greater Short-toed Larks and Lesser Short-toed Larks are already back claiming their territories. Greaters can be seen and heard song flighting in many areas, but to find Lessers your best bet is to visit the area south of the interpretation centre at Castro Marim, where both species breed side by side. In the same area the first of the Spectacled Warblers should have returned and will be singing. Another early returner is the Little Ringed Plover, which will have come back to its favoured shingle banks along the inland rivers.

Fonte de Benemola, near Loulé, is an excellent place to discover the emerging spring flora or perhaps find a rare bird. In wet years the fonte is a bubbling cauldron - a natural Jacuzzi.

93

1st - 15th March - Botanical Climax

Spring days are mostly sunny, sometimes hot, but early mornings can be chilly and are often humid. Sometimes at this time of the year, it rains heavily. The evenings cool rapidly as the sun goes down and so fires are still lit. Occasionally, there are bitingly cold winds from the northern quadrant.

A farm field is transformed into a spectacular wildflower meadow in March.

The timing and intensity of the botanical climax varies considerably from year to year; it seems that everything happens earlier after a wet winter. In a very dry year, spring can pass almost unnoticed until mid April. A good marker of the peak is the full flowering of Gum Cistus *Cistus ladanifer*; then these large white blooms with their maroon and yellow centres spectacularly transform every hillside. Suddenly, the softly rounded hills become a bubbling green sea, the white cistus flowers providing the bubbles.

In places, the gorse *Genista hirsuta* makes a tremendous splash of yellow, as does Shrubby Scorpion Vetch *Coronilla valentina,* which in recent years has moved rapidly westwards along the verges of the A22 motorway. The gorse *Genista tridentatum,* with its orange-yellow flowers, is common on shaley hillsides, while in the higher hills the broom-like Adenocarpus *Adenocarpus complicatus* is in flower.

At this time of year the wildflowers in bloom are too numerous to list but, to select just a few, look out for the delightful Yellow Anemone *Anemone palmata*, the superb fritillary *Fritillaria lusitanica* (let's call it the Portuguese Fritillary), Annual Rockrose *Tuberaria guttata*, Love-in-a-mist *Nigella damascena*, French Lavender *Lavandula stoechas*, the ever-lasting Winged Sea Lavender *Limonium sinuatum*, Wild Jasmine *Jasminum fruticans*, Borage *Borago officinalis* and a whole host of birthworts, mignonettes, poppies, lupins, vetches, lotuses, cistuses, phlomises, mallows, gromwells, alkanets, buglosses, buttercups, violets, periwinkles, valerians, pimpernels, thrifts, toadflaxes and broomrapes.

Especially beautiful is the Portuguese peony Rosa Albardeira *Paeonia broteroi* named after Felix d'Avelar Brotero (1744-1828), Portugal's first professional botanist.

Portuguese Fritillary

Annual Rockrose

Monocotyledons in bloom at this time of year include Spanish Bluebell *Scilla hispanica*, the so-called Brown Bluebell *Dipcadi serotinum*, Common Grape Hyacinth *Muscari neglectum*, Tassel Hyacinth *Muscari comosum*, the squill *Scilla monophyllos*, Sand Crocus *Ornithogalum collinum*, the crocus-like *Romulea bulbocodium* and the beautiful miniature iris Barbary Nut *Gynandriris sisyrinchium*, which blooms only in the afternoon.

Dipcadi fully deserves an oxymoron as its common name: the 'Brown Bluebell'.

Scilla monophyllos, a member of the family Hyacinthaceae. Each flower stem is associated with a single leaf.

On the summit plateau of Rocha da Pena the gorgeous Hoop Petticoat Daffodil *Narcissus bulbocodium* and the tiny daffodil *Narcissus gaditanus* will be showing especially well.

There are also plenty of early orchids to be discovered, including Long-spurred Orchid *Orchis longicornu*, Green-winged Orchid *Anacamptis morio,* Conical Orchid *Orchis conica* and (right) Pyramidal Orchid *Anacamptis pyramidalis.*

Where there is shallow standing or slow-flowing freshwater you can expect to see plenty of Water Crowfoot *Ranunculus* spp and, around the margins, patches of the unusual three-petalled Water-plantain *Alisma plantago-aquatica* pictured below.

The Green-winged Orchid is one of the first grassland orchids to flower.

In the hills listen for the call of the first Cuckoo. Wrens, Blue Rock Thrushes, Chaffinches and Iberian Chiffchaffs are singing, and in the corkwoods Blue Tits, Crested Tits, Nuthatches and Short-toed Treecreepers should be easy enough to find. In these uplands, larger birds are scarce but noisy Jays and Azure-winged Magpies soon make their presence known. Great Spotted Woodpeckers and Lesser Spotted Woodpeckers are drumming, and at night Scops Owls are calling. Wood Pigeons and Turtle Doves are passing through, and the invasive Collared Doves are displaying.

In lowland gardens, Blackbirds, Greenfinches, Goldfinches and Great Tits are singing strongly and Sardinian Warblers are song flighting. On traditionally farmed land and in grasslands, almost impossible-to-see Quails are quietly quipping 'wet my lips, wet my lips', Stone-curlews are eerily calling at night and numerous Corn Buntings are jangling their keys.

White Storks, with their great nests, are very busy. One of the delights of storky towns such as Tavira and Faro is the way in which the crescendo of bill clapping from greeting storks manages to rise above the traffic noise.

A White Stork on its nest waits patiently for the return of its mate.

The first Woodchat Shrikes will be arriving, and in favoured areas such as Azinhal and Castro Marim close to the Rio Guadiana Great Spotted Cuckoos will be chasing each other and seeking out pairs of unfortunate Magpies to be host to their progeny. In the scrubby parts of wetlands, newly arrived male Yellow Wagtails of the distinctive Iberian race, looking like bright yellow orbs, will be staking their claims to territory. If you visit reedbeds listen out for Sedge Warblers, as sometimes they stop to sing as they pass through.

Yellow Wagtail

99

Around midday in the sunshine, many butterflies will be flying. New species to add to the annual list are Southern Scarce Swallowtail, Green Hairstreak, Wood White, Holly Blue, Wall Brown and the introduced Geranium Bronze.

March is when the lovely Southern Scarce Swallowtail first puts in an appearance. Almond trees and other members of the *Prunus* genus are the main food source for its larvae.

The spring sunshine also brings out lizards and snakes to bask on rocks and stone walls. Look out for the huge, green (Ocellated) Eyed Lizard, the well-marked Horseshoe Whip Snake and the uniformly-coloured Ladder Snake. In river pools, Viperine Snakes are easy to spot.

An Algerian Sand Lizard basks in the midday sun.

The Ocellated or Eyed Lizard, the largest lizard found in Europe, grows to an overall length of typically 50cm and exceptionally 90cm; of this the tail makes up about two thirds.

If you are short of time you really must visit a wetland, because there are always some birds to see there - even during this seasonal lull between the departing winter visitors and the arriving passage migrants. However, at this time of year botany rather than ornithology must be the choice for a field trip. Don't waste a day. Put on the walking shoes and head for the hills and cliff tops. Find and follow long forgotten donkey trails. Cross ridges, descend into valleys, explore corkwoods and follow streams until they broaden and meet rivers. Wander the riverbanks and look to the margins of orchards and fields. The wealth of wildflowers is truly amazing.

Cork Oak woodland contains a wealth of wildlife habitat. Even the stacked harvests of cork bark serve as excellent temporary reptile housing.

16th - 31st March - Spring Equinox

The glorious natural climax maintains its pace. Sparklingly, crisp dawns give way to sunny spring mornings and lazy afternoons, but the warm evenings bring out the first of the year's annoying mosquitoes. Of course, strong winds and even storms can occur, but they are the exception rather than the rule.

Oak trees *Quercus* spp are full of downy catkins and bright new leaves, and the shrub-like Mastic Tree *Pistacia lentiscus* has clustered red male flowers with green female flowers below. Pear trees *Pyrus* spp and plum trees *Prunus* spp are in full bloom. Along the roads, Judas Trees *Cercis siliquastrum* are laden with deep-purple flowers, and the planted white iris *Iris albicans* lines the verges. The Judas Tree is said to be the tree from which Judas Iscariot hanged himself and whose flowers blush with shame. In coastal areas and along riverbeds tamarisk trees *Tamarix* spp are beginning to flower. Great swathes of Crown Daisies *Chrysanthemum coronarium* cover bare ground.

French Lavender is in bloom from valley floor to mountain top at this time of year.

In the countryside, the campion *Silene colorata,* Purple Viper's Bugloss *Echium plantagineum,* French Lavender *Lavandula stoechas,* Corn Marigold *Chrysanthemum segetum* and Pale Flax *Linum bienne* dominate the field layer. Fedia *Fedia cornucopiae,* another common carpeting plant, can also be seen now.

The striking salt-loving broomrape Cistanche

Flowering Gum Cistus *Cistus ladanifer* and Small-flowered Gorse *Ulex parviflorus* cover the hillsides. Rue *Ruta graveolens* and Fringed Rue *Ruta chalepensis* are unusual plants also found on hillsides; the dull yellow, dark-centred flowers and bluish-green leaves are distinctive, but the most striking feature is their choking pungency. Rues can blister and pigment bare skin if touched in hot sun. In classical times these plants were valued for their medicinal and aphrodisiac qualities, but nowadays they are used only to flavour grappa, an Italian brandy.

On the salt marshes, the unmistakable yellow cones of Cistanche *Cistanche phelypaea* are in flower; this parasitic broomrape is rather rare outside of the coastal Algarve.

The dominant flower of these marshes in spring is Sand Stock *Malcolmia littorea*. In places, the southern African exotic *Arctotheca calendula*, a purple-centred daisy-like flower, has become naturalised. In damp and sandy habitats look for the spectacular blue heads of *Scilla peruviana* that, despite its name, is a native flower.

On rocky coasts, both Sweet Alison *Lobularia maritima* and Yellow Sea Aster *Asteriscus maritimus* are evident.

The wildflowers at Cabo de São Vicente (Cape St Vincent) are superb, forming an endless rock garden of amazing variety. Most surprising, for visitors to the Algarve, are the full-sized red Snapdragons *Antirrhinum majus*.

Wild Snapdragons

This is the very best time to get out in the countryside and enjoy the spectacular wildflower displays. Cereal fields are not a dull monochrome green in the Algarve, where various types of poppies, daisies and alkanets bloom to provide a succession of colourful flowers right through to harvest time.

The mat-forming Hottentot Figs, which have fleshy leaves and spectacular flowers - either yellow *Carpobrotus edulis* or bright purple *Carpobrotus acinaciformis* - were introduced from South Africa and are now widespread in the Algarve, but unfortunately invasive at the expense of native flora.

After Cabo de São Vicente, the undoubted botanical highlight of an Algarve spring must be the splendid orchids. Careful searching of open woodland and grassy areas, particularly those close to the coast in the west,

Both kinds of Hottentot Fig can occur together.

should be rewarded with finds of several orchid species. These could include the extraordinary Naked Man Orchid *Orchis italica*, Dense-flowered Orchid *Neotinea maculata*, Yellow Bee Orchid *Ophrys lutea*, Bee Orchid *Ophrys apifera*, Bumblebee Orchid *Ophrys bombyliflora*, Mirror Orchid *Ophrys speculum*, Sawfly Orchid *Ophrys tenthredinifera*, Tongue Orchid *Serapias lingua* and the Small-flowered Tongue Orchid *Serapias parviflora*.

The Mirror Orchid *Ophrys speculum* is a star-turn in springtime. The 'speculum' on the lip of the flower glints brilliantly in the spring sunshine, making this an easy orchid to find.

Revitalised by winter rain, the rivers are full of shoaling fish, which in stiller pools attract the attention of Viperine Snakes. In the eastern Algarve many of the fish appear to be the minnow-like Jarubago *Anaecypris hispanica*, which is unique to the Guadiana and Guadalquivir river systems and supposedly facing extinction. Algerian Sand Lizards are active again. Sadly, numerous Western Hedgehog road kills are also indicative of spring activity.

Just waiting to happen...

For the birdwatcher this is also a time of considerable variety. A few winter visitors linger but most have left. Cuckoos are calling and Bee-eaters are passing overhead, but by the month's end they will be investigating their usual colonies. Where there are Magpies, keep an eye open for the Great Spotted Cuckoos that parasitise them. In the hills, Short-toed Eagles and Black-eared Wheatears have returned, and now that the hunters have gone, paired Red-legged Partridges are everywhere.

Spectacled Warbler

At Azinhal, Spectacled Warblers and Dartford Warblers are song flighting, and Zitting Cisticolas 'zip zip zip' monotonously. Here too, one or two male Little Bustards display spectacularly and a pair of Black-shouldered Kites returns briefly every spring. The first Nightingales will be singing, snatchy and subdued at first but full and strong by the month's end. For many species the breeding season is already well advanced. Some pairs of Kentish Plovers on the salinas and Little Ringed Plovers on the rivers will already have chicks. Female Mallards are sitting on eggs or already have ducklings, whilst the drakes (job done!) gather in bachelor parties.

Compared to the autumn, the spring passage is a subdued affair. Nevertheless, Whinchats, Northern Wheatears, Tree Pipits, Willow Warblers, Common Swifts and Pallid Swifts occur widely. Along coastal cliffs keep an eye open for Ring Ouzels, and in damp areas various races of Yellow Wagtail in full plumage. In among the duck flocks look for the distinctive drake Garganey. Black Kites and Marsh Harriers are moving through, and the river valleys attract Green Sandpipers. Audouin's Gulls, Common Terns and a few Gull-billed Terns move along the coast. Offshore, small parties of Common Scoters head westwards and northwards.

Occasionally weather systems blow up from North Africa, and this is a time to be aware that the extraordinary may be swept northwards into the Algarve – for example a White-crowned Black Wheatear, a Ruddy Shelduck or a Trumpeter Finch. The variety and numbers of butterflies are now increasing. The Marsh Fritillary is a local species but can be found easily enough at the Alvor Estuary in late March.

The Marsh Fritillary is easy to find around the Alvor Estuary in March.

If you can drag yourself away from the delights of the Algarve at this time, the place to be is Castro Verde. Everywhere on the steppe-like plains, male Little Bustards are huffing and puffing, jumping up and down and quietly burping. Stately Great Bustards are also there, strutting around in all-male droves; the males perform spectacularly at leks in the early morning and evening, when they turn themselves into huge fluffy white balls that are visible at great distances.

Birds of prey will not disappoint and will certainly include stunning male Montagu's Harriers, Black Kites, Common Buzzards, Lesser Kestrels and Common Kestrels, and possibly Black-shouldered Kite, Red Kite and Bonelli's Eagle. With luck, Black-bellied Sandgrouse will also be there, and in any event the displaying Calandra Larks are superb and they alone would make the journey worthwhile.

1st - 15th April - April Showers

Although many days are gloriously fine and sunny, the early mornings can be grey and cold, sometimes bitterly cold. Chilling winds are not uncommon and April showers are usually not far away. Locals say that if January, February and March have been dry then expect April and perhaps May and even June to be wet. Soon after any rain, the snail collectors are out and about with their buckets, even along the verges of the N 125. Everywhere, the air is full of the heady perfume of flowering orange orchards.

The Japanese Loquat trees *Eriobotrya japonica,* which were introduced from China in the eighteenth century, are now in fruit. Their distinctive yellow fruits are fleshy but contain hard seeds. Known locally as nêsperas, they are delicious when ripe but very acidic if they are picked too soon.

Everywhere the countryside has been transformed into a patchwork quilt of many colours. Small green fields of spring cereals, swathes of Corn Marigolds *Chrysanthemum segetum,* and patches of French Lavender *Lavandula stoechas*, Purple Viper's Bugloss *Echium plantagineum* and the chamomile *Chamaemelum mixtum* interrupt the heaths of gorse and cistus. Meadows and any broken ground will be covered with a riot of wild flowers but dominated by huge patches of Crown Daisy *Chrysanthemum coronarium,* mostly the pale yellow and white variety *discolor.*

Keep a lookout also for Field Gladiolus *Gladiolus italicus*, Tassel Hyacinth *Muscari comosum,* the Star-of-Bethlehem *Ornithogalum narbonense* and Large Cuckoo Pint *Arum italicum,* which show particularly well at this time. The beautiful yellow narcissus Common Jonquil *Narcissus jonquilla* grows locally along riverbanks; this sweet-scented flower is used in perfumery.

Large Cuckoo Pint with green spathe and pale yellow spadix comprising male and female flowers

Apart from the ubiquitous Gum Cistus *Cistus ladanifer*, the cistus family is well represented by other species in flower during April. These include the large white-flowered Poplar-leaved Cistus *Cistus populifolius* and *Cistus palhinhae* from the extreme southwest, the smaller white-flowered Sage-leaved Cistus *Cistus salvifolius* and Narrow-leaved Cistus *Cistus monspeliensis*, the pink-flowered Grey-leaved Cistus *Cistus albidus* and vivid rosy-purple *Cistus crispus*. The yellow-flowered cistuses are the closely-related Halimiums.

Sage-leaved Cistus   **Grey-leaved Cistus**

Look closely where the stems of various kinds of cistus emerge from the ground and you might well see either a bright red-flowered or a bright yellow-flowered parasitic plant. These are *Cytinus hypocistis* and *Cytinus ruber*. In some locations you can find as many as six of these strange bunches of flowers packed around a single cistus bush.

Cytinus hypocistis **has this cistus bush surrounded.**

Except in the intensively populated coastal strip, Nightingales are in full voice. In wooded areas, Nuthatches are suddenly noisy and obvious. Cetti's Warblers concealed in riverside undergrowth explode into song, and Great Reed Warblers grate and croak away among the lakeside vegetation. Montagu's Harriers are back sweeping the open grasslands, and to everybody's delight the first Golden Oriole of the summer will have been spotted.

Spotted Redshank

On the salinas, large numbers of Dunlin sporting smart new black waistcoats are passing through, and with them will be parties of handsome Spotted Redshanks and Bar-tailed Godwits.

Black-winged Stilts and Common Redshanks are copulating and noisily hounding any intruders. Conditions are not always suitable in the salinas, and so the spring shorebird passage can at times lack excitement.

At Castro Marim there are usually Curlew Sandpipers and a few Collared Pratincoles (left).

During the mating season Black-winged Stilts become agressive and territorial.

Emerging butterflies to look out for include Western Dappled White, Black-eyed Blue, Adonis Blue, Southern Brown Argos, Queen of Spain Fritillary, Provençal Fritillary and Spanish Marbled White.

If you get a chance to follow a river valley in the higher hills look out for colonies of the scarce Panoptes Blue.

The distinctive Queen of Spain Fritillary

It's certainly worth journeying into the hills, not only for the wildflowers but also to see the Black-eared Wheatear males of the distinctive Iberian race. These stunning wheatears are common summer visitors to the cistus-covered hills of the eastern Algarve. As a bonus Corn Buntings will be singing everywhere, Thekla Larks will be obvious, and immaculate Woodchat Shrikes, Southern Grey Shrikes and Stonechats and even singing Rock Buntings can be picked out on overhead wires. Other species readily seen in these uplands include Spotless Starling, Azure-winged Magpie and, with a bit of luck, Short-toed Eagle and Raven.

Corn Bunting

16th - 30th April - Bird Show

Late April weather is very variable. The temperature swings from perishingly cold to so hot that it seems as though summer has arrived prematurely. It can rain, and indeed there are years when it does rain steadily. It can be unpleasantly windy, and sometimes from out of nowhere dust devils appear.

Along the roadsides Spanish Broom *Spartium junceum* and Persian Lilac trees *Melia azedarach* are in bloom. The hard seeds of these lilac trees have long been strung together to form rosaries, hence its Portuguese name Conteira. Superb Portuguese cherries appear in the markets and will continue to be available for the next couple of months.

The wildflower show has usually climaxed by now but there is still plenty to enjoy and study. Great carpets of wild Snapdragons *Antirrhinum majus* cover the cliffs of the southwest, where many flowers bloom later and for longer. Several species of the pea family, Fabaceae, are comparatively late flowering and many a happy hour can be spent trying to sort out the huge variety of Algarvian vetches, peas, restharrows, medicks, lotuses and trefoils.

Lathyrus cicera **is just one of the many beautiful vetches that occur in the Algarve.**

113

Bee-eater colonies are now fully active.

Reinforcements of Golden Orioles are arriving, and the Bee-eater colonies are fully active. Cuckoos call, and in a few places the bizarre Great Spotted Cuckoo will still be seeking out its host species, which in the Algarve include Azure-winged Magpies and Southern Grey Shrikes. The Magpie is its preferred foster parent, but this is an uncommon bird so far south.

In the woodlands, Blackcaps and Chaffinches endeavour to compete in song with Nightingales, and in the valleys the scratchy song of the Melodious Warbler hardly justifies its name. Where there are rock faces, look for Rock Buntings and singing and displaying Blue Rock Thrushes.

Locally, pairs of Cirl Buntings will have returned to their haunts. In the feeding flocks of hirundines, especially over water, look out for Sand Martins on passage.

Southern Grey Shrike

As ever, the coastal wetlands provide a tremendous show of birds. Male Yellow Wagtails look immaculate in their bright yellow garb. At Castro Marim, Spectacled Warblers are singing and both Greater Short-toed Larks and Lesser Short-toed Larks are song flighting. The numbers of Greater Flamingos - sometimes more than a thousand at Castro Marim - and Spoonbills are now peaking. A good number and variety of shorebirds and a few raptors are passing through. This is a great time to locate Ruff.

Little Terns have returned in strength, whereas Sandwich Terns are leaving. Superb, fully plumaged Black Terns, looking like giant insects, stop briefly to rest and feed daintily. Specialist bird tour groups arrive from the north to feast their eyes on the exciting array of breeding birds and to enjoy the spectacle of the wetlands. If they are lucky, they will have stories to tell of rare spring migrants and possibly vagrants too.

A Little Tern heads off for its lunch.

Both the Southern Gatekeeper (above) and its less widely distributed relative the Spanish Gatekeeper occur in the Algarve.

More and more butterflies are appearing, including the tropical looking Two-tailed Pasha, the more mundane Southern Gatekeeper and several confusing skippers. On the summit plateau of Rocha da Pena, the Marsh Fritillary is now in flight.

Mammals have young to feed and so they are more active at this time of the year. Even nocturnal species, such as the Wildcat and Red Fox venture forth in daylight to feed their young, and so they are more likely to be seen at this time. Sunny days will see lizards and snakes active.

In springtime Red Foxes hunt by night and by day to find enough food for their young.

Study the map and find a quieter crossing of one of the larger rivers, such as the Vascão or Foupana, and spend the day enjoying the rich variety of birds, flowers and butterflies along the banks. Take a picnic and siesta to the sounds of nature.

1st - 15th May - A Watch of Nightingales

This is a delightful time of year. Everywhere there are plenty of wildflowers to enjoy. Butterflies are numerous and the species diversity is at its best. However, be warned that on May Day (1st May) - Dia do Trabalhador - everybody goes into the countryside, especially where there is running water, to embrace the greenery and enjoy a barbecue or a picnic. Traditionally, snails are eaten on this day. Early May mornings are usually cool enough to induce enthusiasm for a good walk and the afternoons hot enough to warrant just relaxing and contemplating the morning's exertions. Occasional days are cloudy and in some years it does rain but usually not for too long. In wet years, the upside is that seasonal rivers will have a good flow, making them splendid places to visit to see wildlife.

Early in the spring, rivers have plenty of flow and are resplendent with Water Crowfoot.

Many gardens have Apricot trees *Prunus armeniaca* and they will be laden with ripe fruit for just a few days. Algarvian apricots are superb and make wonderful jam. Home-grown apricots always taste so much better than the bland varieties sold in supermarkets.

The delightful Little Ringed Plover

Melodious Warbler

Rufous-tailed Scrub Robins are just returning to the eastern river valleys. Along these valleys, Little Ringed Plover, Common Sandpiper, Kingfisher, Grey Wagtail and Cetti's Warbler are breeding and it seems that under almost every bridge a pair of Red-rumped Swallows is constructing a bottle-shaped nest.

Crag Martins have in recent years colonised many of the newly constructed road bridges in the eastern Algarve. Nightingales, Melodious Warblers and Blackcaps sing everywhere.

In more open country, it is a good time to detect and learn the songs of Rock Bunting, Blue Rock Thrush and the handsome Black-eared Wheatear. In the Cork Oak woodland, try and locate the canopy-loving Orphean Warbler by listening for its distinctive song. Two other speciality breeding species in these woodlands that are well worth seeking out are Common Redstart and Hawfinch. Chaffinches will be singing strongly, and in open woodland look for Subalpine Warbler, Crested Tit, Nuthatch, Short-toed Treecreeper and Lesser Spotted Woodpecker.

The handsome Black-eared Wheatear

The Wryneck (pictured on the right) also occurs in the Algarve. These extraordinary birds, closely related to the woodpeckers, are thinly distributed; however, when they are present they are readily located by their ringing but plaintive calls.

The beginning of May is the best time in spring to see such passerine migrants as Spotted Flycatcher, Pied Flycatcher and Common Redstart. Short-toed Eagles, Montagu's Harriers, Common Buzzards, Common Kestrels and occasionally Booted Eagles and Black-shouldered Kites can be seen hunting; and at night, listen for Red-necked Nightjar, Stone-curlew, Tawny Owl and Scops Owl and, of course, Nightingale. Little Owls are as noisy as ever at dawn and dusk.

Early May is a good time to see Montagu's Harrier.

Nearly all of the waders in the wetlands are in spanking field-guide plumage, so there is no better time to begin lesson one in shorebird identification. Some of the Ruffs passing through are quite breathtaking, too, and the Knots are in full red rig. Not to be left out, Black Terns show just what can be done in monochrome.

Rare waders occasionally turn up in the spring, when they are far easier to identify. Keep in mind the possibility of seeing such species as Pectoral Sandpiper, Marsh Sandpiper, Red-necked Phalarope and even Lesser Yellowlegs.

Marsh Sandpiper

Lizards and snakes are now wide-awake and frogs are in full voice. The larger number of road kills sadly evidences the increased mammal activity. Although grisly, these kills are often the only way to determine the presence of secretive nocturnal species.

Frogs, including the Mediterranean Tree Frog, are in full voice at this time of the year.

The Iberian Water Frog is also more active now.

On the lakes at Ludo and São Lourenço, Purple Gallinules, Coots and Moorhens will have downy young, and ducklings follow adult Mallard, Gadwall and Red-crested Pochards. With patience, Little Bitterns and even Purple Herons will be seen, and Great Reed Warblers can be heard singing from lakeside vegetation.

The Purple Heron is a very patient bird, standing as still as a statue on the edge of a swamp and waiting for its food to arrive by water, land or air. Like other herons, its diet consists mainly of fish, amphibians and invertebrates, but this opportunist feeder will also take advantage of any lizards or insects that come just that little bit too close for comfort.

16th - 31st May - Prelude to Summer

Although becoming steadily hotter, the weather is still cool enough around dawn to entice the naturalist out of bed. Late May can sometimes be cloudy and rain is still a possibility. Summer is almost here. Trails are now shared with early morning joggers and cyclists, jet skis scream up and down the beaches and lagoons, and sometimes micro-light aircraft playfully buzz both birds and birdwatchers. Beautiful, blue-flowered Jacaranda trees *Jacaranda mimosifolia* bloom spectacularly in the towns.

Tavira, where the Jacaranda Trees are at their very best in late May

Andryala

In the countryside Pomegranate trees *Punica granatum* are covered in waxy red flowers. Three of the most obvious flowers covering roadside verges and disturbed ground are the strikingly pale yellow Andryala *Andryala integrifolia* - Camaraira in Portuguese - the sticky pea-flowered Large Yellow Rest-harrow *Ononis natrix* and the huge yellow umbellifer Giant Fennel *Ferula communis*.

Along roadsides in the hills *Helichrysum stoechas* (above), smelling strongly of curry, is in flower, and the rangy Spanish Oyster Plant (below) is almost everywhere.

Broad-leaved Helleborines are found in woodlands throughout the Algarve. There is rarely any need to wander away from paths because these late-blooming orchids are most abundant beside such well trodden ways.

As the seas of cistus lose their colour, yellow bushes of the broom-like Lygos *Lygos sphaerocarpa* appear like shafts of sunlight. This is also a good time to get to know your onions. The large dark purple-red globular flowers of Round-headed Leek *Allium sphaerocephalon* stand proud in cornfields, while Rosy Garlic *Allium roseum* flowers in the margins. Close to the coast and along riverbanks look out for the attractive *Allium subvillosum* and Wild Leek *Allium ampeloprasum.*

On the Tavira salinas, Kentish Plovers, Avocets, Black-winged Stilts, Common Redshanks and Little Terns have young. Purple Herons are regularly seen at Ludo and probably breed there. Woodlarks are widespread inland, where their outstanding song is often uttered during a circular song flight. Late migrants are still dribbling through and if you are very lucky you might even see a Roller.

Roller

This is perhaps the best time of all for butterflies. As well as listing the usual species, try and sort out the Long-tailed Blue from Lang's Short-tailed Blue - both are widespread. Overlooked or local species to track down are Adonis Blue, Spanish Fritillary, Aethrie Fritillary, Spanish Gatekeeper, Red-underwing Skipper and Lulworth Skipper.

Sorting out the various Blues can be very challenging. The Common Blue has distinctive orange spots on the underwing.

Paired butterflies are not only much easier to photograph, but seeing the markings on male and female helps with identification.

Spring stays longer in the Algarve hills, and so this is a good time to get out and explore the very attractive area around Monchique. There the wealth of wildflowers will still be obvious. Plants that enjoy a more temperate climate are in bloom - for example the native rhododendron *Rhododendron ponticum.*

Look there also for such birds as the Robin, Firecrest and Spotted Flycatcher, because in summer they do not occur elsewhere in the Algarve.

Spotted Flycatcher

A few pairs of the scarce Little Bustard still breed in the remoter grasslands and open heathland of the Algarve.

1st - 15th June - Long Summer Days

The days are mostly sunny and dry but the early mornings are cool enough and occasionally a touch grey and overcast. Sudden summer storms and showers sometimes bring much needed rain. As the day wears on, heat haze can become a problem and the azure blue seascapes become eggshell blue. The long evenings are perfect for barbecues.

There is plenty of good fruit in the markets including the first local plums, peaches, nectarines and figs. Portuguese figs are regarded by many as the best in the world.

In the hills, the steep grain fields are still painstakingly scythed by hand. As the land dries, so wildflowers become fewer but Oleander *Nerium oleander* is appearing and the striking, large-headed Rough-leaved Globe-thistle *Echinops strigosus* is in bloom. In the fallow fields there are still plenty of flowers. Among the numerous yellow Asteraceae, Tolpis *Tolpis barbata* is easily identified by its dark reddish-purple centre and square-cut petals.

Thistles continue to bloom in the hot summer days long after most flowers have given up.

Most songbirds are still singing and some are song flighting. Cuckoos continue to call but they will not do so for much longer. At dusk, the strange rhythmic knocking of the Red-necked Nightjars can be heard.

Seasonal rivers are drying rapidly, leaving behind nutrient-rich pools that are often covered with mats of green algae. Along valleys and gullies in the eastern Algarve, displaying Rufous-tailed Scrub Robins spread their wings and seemingly turn themselves inside out. They cock their fanned tails right over their heads and pump them vigorously. The broad black-and-white tail is an important part of the display, the feather tips contrasting sharply with the bright orange-rufous tail base.

Ribeira Odeleite. In summer the rivers become nutrient rich, and some cease to flow at all, becoming pools of concentrated wildlife and a magnet for thirsty animals and birds.

Little Terns are late breeders and are actively feeding along most of the shoreline and up into the tidal estuaries and rivers. The rare Audouin's Gull is a recent colonist in the Algarve. A few Audouin's Gulls, Mediterranean Gulls, Slender-billed Gulls and Gull-billed Terns move along the coast in early June, and occasionally among them are adult Lesser Black-backed Gulls with truly black backs.

Slender-billed Gulls occur regularly at Castro Marim in June.

The gorgeous Curlew Sandpiper

On the marshes, a few superbly plumaged migrant waders are still passing through; in particular, keep a look out for the gorgeous Curlew Sandpipers.

Oddly, small parties of Grey Plovers in non-breeding plumage are appearing, and large numbers of Black-tailed Godwits are gathering even at this late date. These are either non-breeding birds or failed breeding birds returning from the north.

Grey Plover

Egyptian Mongooses are more active now and can often be seen in daylight. Unfortunately the hunting fraternity considers these animals a threat to game, and they set large steel traps to catch them. Huge, green Eyed Lizards are occasionally disturbed.

Smaller lizards usually see or hear you and dart away long before you get a chance to see them. This is particularly so in woodlands, where it is impossible to move about silently because of the inevitable crunching of twigs and dry leaves beneath your feet.

There is a good variety of butterflies, and this is a good time to sort out the hairstreaks and fritillaries that are widespread but have only a brief flight period.

The striking Black-veined White is one of the Algarve's most sought after butterflies and is best looked for where Almond trees occur.

The rare Spotted Fritillary is confined to coastal areas of the Algarve.

Summer heat arrives suddenly and induces lethargy. Then, a novel way to enjoy the Algarvian countryside is to take the train. A local line runs from the Spanish border at Vila Real de Santo António to Faro and from Faro to Lagos in the west. The trains are inexpensive, infrequent and slow but never crowded; they provide a leisurely way to enjoy the scenic contrasts of the Algarvian littoral. Especially interesting is the journey through the Parque Natural da Ria Formosa between Tavira and Faro, where on the seaward side glimpses of a good variety of wetland birds are guaranteed.

16th - 30th June - Summer Equinox

Days are long and it is after nine before the sun goes down. Do not waste the day. Get up and take a walk before breakfast: enjoy nature at its best. Often the weather is perfect. Dusk and dawn are cool but the days are hot and sunny, sometimes too hot to do much after lunch. Mornings can be cloudy but it is not long before the sun takes control. For the residents, daily watering and siestas are a way of life.

In the lowlands, wildflowers are finishing but Wild Carrot *Daucus carota* and the brilliant blue thistle *Cynara algarbiensis* - a smaller version of the huge Cardoon Thistle *Cynara cardunculus* - thrive in the dry conditions. Look for the delicate pink *Dianthus superba* with its distinctively fringed petals, the thin-stemmed bright yellow flax *Linum* sp and the fleshier pale-yellow stonecrop *Sedum sediforme*.

The white head of Wild Carrot often contains a single central purple flower that mimics a fly and encourages pollination by insects.

Helichrysums are shrubby perennials with clusters of yellow flowerheads and are difficult to identify, but *Helichrysum stoechas* is unmistakably curry scented. The tall, striking yellow flower with a prominent purple centre that appears in patches along roadsides is the mullein *Verbascum sinuatum*.

135

In the Barrocal, Oleander *Nerium oleander* is showing well and bushy clumps of the thyme *Thymus capitatus* are everywhere. Common Myrtle *Myrtus communis* is in flower and on Tavira Day, 24th June (Dia de São João) the streets are bedecked with flowering branches. Myrtle has been a symbol of love and peace since classical times and the bark, leaves and flowers contain aromatic oil, Eau d'Agnes, used medicinally and in perfumery.

Common Centaury can flower at almost any time of the year, including in high summer.

Along the roadsides in the hills, the pretty Common Centaury *Centaurium erythraea* - Estrela das Montanhas to the Portuguese - is in flower, and around Monchique huge spikes of flowering Foxgloves *Digitalis purpurea* are almost everywhere. On the higher ground, locals collect flowering Marjoram *Origanum vulgare* to dry and use as a culinary herb.

The beautiful wild peony *Paeonia broteroi*

Blackcaps and Greenfinches are still in song, and much of their activity consists of busy parents attending fledglings; the wetlands around Ludo and Quinta do Lago, Tavira and Castro Marim are bursting with juveniles. With them will be a good selection of wetland birds, many of which are non-breeding loafers or shorebirds such as Black-tailed Godwits already returning south from their northerly breeding grounds. It really is worth making the effort to get out.

Black-tailed Godwits

In river valleys in the north-eastern Algarve, and probably elsewhere, a few pairs of the very rare White-rumped Swift are prospecting active Red-rumped Swallows' nests with a view to occupying them and breeding there. Even if the swifts do not show, these valleys concentrate natural activity.

White-rumped Swifts are prospecting active Red-rumped Swallows' nests with a view to occupying them and breeding there themselves.

Sit concealed in the shade by a river pool and watch what happens. Iberian Water Frogs, terrapins and harmless Viperine Snakes will appear, and various birds come to drink. If it is early enough, a vixen and her half-grown cubs might visit.

Spanish Terrapin

As the sun warms the air, butterflies become numerous. Roadside verges attract interesting skippers and such species as Small Copper, Southern Gatekeeper and Dusky Heath.

The Foupana at Redonda, the Vascão at Giões and the Odeleite at Fortes and Monte da Ribeira are home to a great variety of wildlife. They are wonderful places to have a picnic, and a splash in freshwater makes a change from the beach.

The Ribeira Odeleite at Fortes is a great place for a picnic.

1st - 15th July - Hot Summer

At this time of year it rarely rains and mostly the sun shines. Occasionally it is unbearably hot, with temperatures entering the forties in the shade, but nevertheless some early mornings are cool, grey and overcast.

Not many wildflowers are left in the brown and green countryside, but Oleander *Nerium oleander* is in bloom and Myrtle bushes *Myrtus communis* remain in flower. Here and there the climber Fragrant Clematis *Clematis flammula* forms pretty clumps, and purple patches of bugloss *Echium* sp and thyme *Thymus* sp survive. Wild Carrot *Daucus carota* is a typical Apiaceae, but it is late flowering and its white heads are on broken ground everywhere.

Scilla peruviana. Despite its name this spring wildflower is native to the Algarve.

On the sand dunes and barrier islands, the carpeting yellow flower smelling of curry is *Helichrysum stoechas*. Also in this habitat are the beautiful Sea Daffodil *Pancratium maritimum,* Sea Holly *Eryngium maritimum* and the hardy, heather-like, flowers of Sea Heath *Frankenia* sp. Inland along country lanes, Bear's Breech *Acanthus mollis* is in flower. The distinctive leaf-shape of this plant is found in the motifs on the capitals of Corinthian columns in Ancient Greece.

Sea Holly is one of the few late-flowering umbellifers found on the coastal sand dunes.

On the wetlands, determined birdwatchers can see summering species such as White Stork, Black-winged Stilt, Avocet, Common Redshank, Kentish Plover, Little Tern and Yellow Wagtail. Also present is a good array of visiting birds including Greater Flamingo, Spoonbill and shorebirds, such as Black-tailed Godwit, Grey Plover, Dunlin, Turnstone and Whimbrel.

Whimbrels visit the Algarve at this time of the year.

A stay in the country and time spent exploring valleys and woodland should be rewarded with Bee-eater, all three woodpeckers, Rufous-tailed Scrub Robin, Melodious Warbler, Orphean Warbler, Iberian Chiffchaff, Short-toed Treecreeper, Crested Tit, Spotless Starling, Golden Oriole, Woodchat Shrike, Azure-winged Magpie and Short-toed Eagle.

Among the nocturnally calling species are Red-necked Nightjar, Barn Owl, Tawny Owl and Scops Owl. Even Eagle Owls can sometimes be seen at dusk.

Short-toed Eagle

141

Get up early and catch the first ferry to one of the barrier islands of the Ria Formosa and explore the sand dunes, but keep to the trails. The flora is fascinating and the birds include terns, Kentish Plovers, larks and finches. When it is too hot, take to the sea or simply enjoy a fish lunch and relax.

Kentish Plover

There is still a good show of butterflies, including the Swallowtail (pictured on the right) and the Southern Scarce Swallowtail. Recently emerged Southern Gatekeepers should also be in evidence.

16th - 31st July - Siesta

The Algarvian summer has truly arrived but dawn is always pleasantly cool for an hour or two. The sky, which a few days ago was sharply blue, is now a hazy blue-grey. Hot sandy winds from the Sahara can make it blazing hot and lifeless with temperatures soaring to the mid forties. It almost never rains, but when it does expect splodgy mud falling from the skies that will make parked cars and poolside beds filthy. But on good days, breezes take the heat out of the afternoon air and sometimes evening winds become chilly - then alfresco dining demands a light sweater.

On the coast sun worshippers have returned in force, but not far inland peace and tranquillity reign and the rhythm of life continues largely undisturbed. Hay is cut and baled. But there is uneasiness because the threat of hill fires is never far away. In some years the hinterland is helplessly alight and there is little that os bombeiros can do except watch. Hilltop villas in the Algarvian serras are proliferating because they afford their occupants space and superb views; summer bushfires can destroy everything.

In the markets, a good variety of fruit is on sale to take to the beach including nectarines, peaches and uvas cardinal, the first eating grapes to ripen in the Algarve.

Despite the lateness of the season, interesting birds are still to be found. In the larger river valleys of the eastern Algarve, Rufous-tailed Scrub Robins are busy and obvious. Although the rivers no longer flow, the riverbeds hold deep pools full of fish, and in remote areas Otters are easier to see. Along these stony tracts Little Ringed Plovers, Common Sandpipers, Kingfishers, White Wagtails and Grey Wagtails are still busy feeding their young. Under bridges Crag Martins, House Martins, Red-rumped Swallows and even White-rumped Swifts attend to juveniles. Migrating Green Sandpipers are already moving along these inland valleys.

In high summer, Grey Mullet often move into the brackish lower reaches of rivers.

Away from the valleys the land is arid, but the trees remain green. Even at dawn in the lowlands only a few birds make themselves known, and by mid afternoon all will be silent. Occasionally a family of Woodchat Shrikes moves through the olive trees, and then the air is filled with the incessant cries of the young demanding food from their tireless parents. Sardinian Warblers - in the undergrowth as ever - join in with their sharp irritated chatter.

A butterfly falls prey to a Sardinian Warbler.

As the sun sinks and loses its heat, small flocks of finches feed on grass and thistle heads, while in the orchards tits and treecreepers become active. Swallows, martins and even swifts swoop down to swimming pools.

Blackbirds (left) are the last diurnal birds to settle, but it is now long past the season when we can expect to hear them singing.

Early in the morning, migrating Bee-eaters fly over, their distinctive 'pruutt' calls warning of their approach. Now and again an exotic Hoopoe will visit a well-watered lawn to probe. Shy Turtle Doves are rarely seen but their unusual telephone-like 'turr-turr' (hence the name) can often be heard. In areas with fruiting fig trees, delightfully gaudy Golden Orioles, Jays and Azure-winged Magpies visit. There are plenty of young Rabbits; and Iberian Hares and Western Hedgehogs can also be seen on the move.

The regular watering of golf courses ensures a plentiful supply of food for Hoopoes, which are regular visitors.

Purple Gallinules are easy to see at Quinta do Lago.

On the wetlands Kentish Plovers, Avocets, Black-winged Stilts and Little Terns attend to their young, and on the coastal dunes of the Sotavento showy clumps of Sea Daffodil *Pancratium maritimum* still bloom. Autumn migration has begun, with a good variety of shorebirds.

The leaves of Sea Daffodils remain green until late summer, when they turn brown just as the flowers are ready to open.

Not truly a daffodil, *Pancratium maritimum* is a member of the family Amaryllidaceae. This amazing wildflower thrives in the salt-laden sand right up to the littoral line.

This lovely plant is propagated by large black seeds that are blown across the beach by the wind (or kicked by people). For pollination it depends on a night-flying hawkmoth; the flowers are open from late afternoon through the night and into the next morning.

The lovely Sea Daffodil at close quarters

Visiting Common Redshanks pass through in good numbers, Black-tailed Godwits gather by the hundred, and at high tide groups of tortoiseshell-coloured Turnstones congregate on salinas cross bunds. On sapal and at the margins of salinas, Stone-curlews move around in loose flocks, making them easier to see. At Castro Marim and in the Ria Formosa visiting Collared Pratincoles and Black Terns are moving through. In villa gardens unexpected passerines that are dispersing southwards after breeding occur; you might see Melodious Warblers or a Nightingale feeding under a hedge.

Black-tailed Godwits

A lazy summer is making way for a busy early autumn, and so the year has turned full circle.

Turnstones will soon start to congregate on the salinas.

The Paper Wasp with its intricate nest – one more of the Algarve's amazing inhabitants

Recommended Reading

This book is just an introduction to the wealth of wildlife in the Algarve. It points visitors and Algarvians in the right direction and suggests what they might be able to see. However, to identify with certainty many of the species it is necessary to delve into field guides. Unfortunately the Algarve is not yet blessed with a wealth of regional guides, and so it may be necessary to refer to general European guides, which can result in more confusion than clarity. Here are brief details of some of the books that we can recommend:

General Reading
Algarve Plants and Landscape by D. J. Mabberley and P. J. Placito (Oxford University Press, 1993. ISBN-13: 978-0198587026) is essential reading for anybody interested in the Algarvian countryside and, in particular, its rapidly vanishing traditional way of life.

Birdlife
Although it may not seem so in the middle of a hot summer's day, the Algarve has a great wealth of birdlife. One of the advantages of living in Europe is the large number of books readily available on all aspects of birdwatching - from basic field guides to voluminous works covering all characteristics of every species recorded in Europe. Which field guide should you try to acquire, then?

Collins Bird Guide by Lars Svensson, Killian Mullarney, Dan Zetterstrom and Peter J Grant (Collins, Revised 2nd Edition Sept 2009. ISBN-13: 978-0007267262) is lauded as the best ever European field guide. The illustrations are plentiful and accurate, but the text has little information on jizz, those special non-plumage characteristics that help identification.

Birds of Europe by Lars Jonsson (Christopher Helm, 1992, Re-issue Edition 2005. ISBN-13: 978-0713676006) is very user-friendly. The paintings are bold and lifelike and the words straightforward.

Mammals
Unfortunately, most of the Algarve's mammals are nocturnal and not often seen by the casual visitor. Only hedgehogs, rabbits, hares and various bats, which mostly defy field identification, are readily visible. In remoter districts those seeking wildlife might, if they are lucky, glimpse a fox, an otter or even a party of foraging wild boar. Two well-established North African species are Common Genet, a spotted catlike carnivore and the Egyptian Mongoose. Whilst genets spend the day hiding, mongooses are diurnal and quite commonly seen. Most of the larger terrestrial mammals are unmistakable. Smaller mammals usually come in the form of specimens, perhaps a small vole from a swimming pool filter or just something the cat brought in - then a good reference source is necessary. Although not for the squeamish, road kills provide valuable information on occurrence and distribution.

Collins Field Guide *Mammals of Britain & Europe* by David Macdonald and Priscilla Barrett (Collins, 1993. ISBN-13: 978-0002197793) is a useful and readily available reference book.

The Hamlyn Guide *Bats of Britain and Europe* by Wilfried Schober and Eckard Grimmberger (Hamlyn, 1993. ISBN-13: 978-0600579656) is comprehensive.

Sea Mammals of the World by Randall R. Reeves, Brent S. Stewart, Phillip J. Clapham and James A. Powell (A & C Black, 2002. ISBN-13: 978-0713663341) is splendidly illustrated and a mine of information.

Reptiles and Amphibians
For most visitors the first contact with reptiles is a gecko stalking flies on a villa wall or a dark snake slithering across the road in front of a car. As for amphibians, at night wherever there is freshwater frogs croak in chorus and occasionally a huge female toad, the size of a small football, will amble unconcernedly across a lawn. Unforgettable will be the first meeting with a slow moving, bug-eyed chameleon. This remarkable animal ignores its watchers and just goes about its business of stalking and catching insects with its extraordinary, extensible, pink, sticky tongue. The Algarve is a place to enjoy and learn from such chance encounters. It is not a place to fear reptiles and amphibians. In fact, people say there are no poisonous snakes in Portugal but that is not quite true. Europe has few field guides to its reptiles and amphibians.

Collins Field Guide *Reptiles and Amphibians of Britain and Europe* by Nick Arnold and Denys Ovenden (Collins, 2002. ISBN-13: 978-0002199643) is useful but not comprehensive.

Amphibians and Reptiles of Portugal, Madeira and the Azores-Archipelago by Rudolf Malkmus (A R G Gantner Verlag, 2004. ISBN-13: 978-3-904144-89-6) provides photographs and distributional information.

Butterflies
Although not always obvious, the Algarve plays host to a good variety of butterflies (about 80 species). Due to its geographical position the selection of butterflies is varied: some are common and widespread throughout Europe, others are Mediterranean species, and a few are at the northern limit of their range and therefore more common in North Africa.

As Borboletas de Portugal, edited by Ernestino Maravalhas and published in Portuguese is by far the best book on butterflies in Portugal (Vento Norte, 2003. ISBN-10: 972-96031-9-7).

The Collins Field Guide *Butterflies of Britain & Europe* by Tom Tolman (1997; new edition 2008. ISBN-13: 978-0007242344) is the most authoritative of several excellent European field guides covering butterflies.

Photographic Guide to the Butterflies of Britain & Europe, also by Tom Tolman, (Oxford University Press, 2001. ISBN-13: 978-0198506072) is a useful book with illustrations of butterflies as they appear in the field.

Butterflies by Paul Whalley (Mitchell Beazley, 2000. ISBN-13: 978-1840002720) is a handy pocket guide that covers nearly all of the Algarve's butterflies.

Dragonflies and Damselflies
More people are taking an interest in dragonflies, but they are little studied in the Algarve.

Field Guide to the Dragonflies of Britain and Europe by Klaas-Douwe B Dijkstra (British Wildlife Publishing, 2006. ISBN-13: 978-0953139941) covers all dragonflies and damselflies from the Arctic to the Sahara.

Wildflowers
There is no comprehensive field guide to the wildflowers of the Algarve, but general Mediterranean guides do incorporate southern Portugal. Unfortunately, being an appendage to the Mediterranean, the Algarve is not particularly well served, and this is especially true of endemic or near endemic species.

Wildflowers in the Algarve by Pat O'Reilly and Sue Parker (First Nature, 2008. ISBN-13: 978-0954955496) is a useful introduction to the wealth of Algarve wildflowers; the stunning photographs would encourage anyone to visit the Algarve early in the year.

Mediterranean Wild Flowers by Marjorie Blamey and Christopher Grey-Wilson (HarperCollins, 1993; 2nd Revised Edition 2004. ISBN-13: 978-0713670158) is the best comprehensive regional guide. Most of the names used here follow this guide.

Other general guides covering some of the local species are:

Eyewitness Handbook *Wild Flowers of the Mediterranean* by David Burnie (Eyewitness, 1995. ISBN-13: 978-0751310115)

Field Guide to Wild Flowers of Southern Europe by Paul Davies and Bob Gibbons (The Crowood Press, 1993. ISBN-13: 978-1852236595).

Collins Photoguide to the Wild Flowers of the Mediterranean by Ingrid & Peter Schönfelder (Collins, 1990. ISBN-10: ISBN: 0 00 219863-0)

Flowers of South-west Europe by Oleg Pulunin and B.E. Smythies (Oxford University Press, 1990. ISBN-13: 978-0192881786). This authoritative book provides a detailed overview with some good photographs, but it is hardly a field guide.

Much easier to use but still far from comprehensive are the small handbooks written and privately published by Mary McMutrie between 1973 and 1998: *Wild Flowers of the Algarve, More Wild Flowers of the Algarve, Wild Flowers of the Algarve Books III & IV, Shrubs of the Algarve* and *Trees of Portugal*. It is well worth trying to acquire these attractive and inexpensive little books and also her *Plantas do Algarve*, which was co-authored by M. Alfonso (Serviço Nacional de Parques, 1992. ISBN-10: 9729034451)

Wild Orchids in the Algarve by Sue Parker (First Nature, 2009. ISBN 978-0-9560544-2-5) is a concise illustrated book covering most if not all of the orchid species found in the Algarve.

Orchids of Europe, North Africa and the Middle East by Pierre Delforge (A & C Black, 2006. ISBN-13: 978-0713675252) is comprehensive, although it does not include Algarve-specific information.

Fungi
There are numerous guides available to help with the identification of mushrooms and toadstools, ranging from the highly technical to simple and more reader-friendly books.

Field Guide Mushrooms & Toadstools of Britain & Europe by R. Courtecuisse & B. Duhem (Collins, 1994. ISBN-10: 0002200252) falls into the highly technical category.

Kingfisher Field Guide to the Mushrooms & Toadstools of Britain & Europe by David Pegler (Kingfisher Books Ltd, 1990. ISBN-13: 978-0862725655)

Multimedia Guide to the Kingdom of Fungi by Pat O'Reilly (First Nature, 2008. ISBN-13: 978-0-95695560544-0-1) is an interactive CD-ROM for PCs. Acclaimed for its photography and a wealth of information on many of the world's most beautiful, valuable and dangerous fungi, this interactive CD runs on PCs with Internet Explorer. With more than 1000 high-quality images, detailed identification guides, quizzes, animations and videos plus fascinating facts and myths relating to fungi, this is a useful non-technical introduction to the subject.

Griffon Vultures

Index of Scientific Names
Figures refer to page numbers; pictures are denoted by bold text page numbers.

Indexes

Index of Common Names
Figures refer to page numbers; pictures are denoted by bold text page numbers.

Birds

Accentor, Alpine 65, **81**
Avocet 15, 19, **23**, 26, 33, 127, 141, 146
Bee-eater 19, 106, **114**, 141, 145
Bittern, Little 15, 123 499, **145**
Blackbird **144**
Blackcap 23, 44, 64, 69, 73, 114, 118, 137
Bluethroat 33, 65, **75**
Brambling 64
Bullfinch 64
Bunting, Cirl 53, 80, 114
Bunting, Corn 35, 37, 58, 73, 99, **112**
Bunting, Rock 73, 112, 114, 119
Bunting, Snow 81
Bustard, Great 107
Bustard, Little 15, 40, **53**, 106, 107, **129**
Buzzard, Common 30, 31, 32, 45, 65, 74, 86, 107, 120
Buzzard, Honey 31
Buzzard, Long-legged 86
Chaffinch 64, 98, 114, 119
Chiffchaff, Common 25, 58, **64**, 69, 73
Chiffchaff, Iberian 20, 73, 92, 98, 141
Chough, Red-billed 38
Cisticola, Zitting **25**, 106
Coot 123
Cormorant 47
Crow, Carrion 38
Cuckoo 98, 106, 114, 130
Cuckoo, Great Spotted 99, 106
Curlew 15
Dove, Collared 98
Dove, Turtle 18, 98, 145

Duck, Tufted 40, 80
Dunlin 15, 59, 65, 110, 141
Dunnock 44, 65, 69
Eagle, Bonelli's 31, 38, 107
Eagle, Booted 31, 38, 45, 54, 74, 120
Eagle, Short-toed 31, 38, 45, 106, 112, 120, **141**
Egret, Cattle **161**
Egret, Little 15, 33, **60**
Falcon, Peregrine 38, 65, 74
Fieldfare 65, 69
Finch, Snow 81
Firecrest 44, 58, 80, 128
Flamingo, Greater **4**, 15, 19, 26, 33, **40**, 53, 92, 115, 141
Flycatcher, Pied 19, **25**, 34, 47, 52, 120
Flycatcher, Spotted 25, 34, 47, 120, **128**
Gadwall 15, 40, 80, 123
Gallinule, Purple 15, 123, **145**
Gannet 9, 21, 34
Garganey 26, 106
Godwit, Bar-tailed 15, 41, 47, **59**, 65, 110
Godwit, Black-tailed 15, 19, 26, 33, 59, 75, 92, 132, **137**, 141, **147**
Goldcrest 80
Goldfinch 37, **52**, 64, 99
Goose, Greylag 59, **85**
Goshawk 38
Grebe, Black-necked 47, **92**
Grebe, Great Crested 15, 92
Grebe, Little 47, 92
Greenfinch 64, 99, 137
Greenshank 15, 41, 65
Gull, Audouin's 15, 33, **41**, 59, 65, 106, 131
Gull, Black-headed 15

Gull, Glaucous 81
Gull, Herring 16, 65
Gull, Lesser Black-backed **16**, 65, 131
Gull, Little **47**
Gull, Mediterranean 33, 131
Gull, Slender-billed 65, 70, **131**
Gull, Yellow-legged 16, 65
Harrier, Hen 31, 38, 58, 65, 74
Harrier, Marsh 31, 38, 65, **86**, 106
Harrier, Montagu's 19, 26, 31, 107, 110, **120**
Heron, Grey 15
Heron, Purple 15, **123**, 127
Hobby 31, 45
Hoopoe 9, **58**, 92
Ibis, Glossy 15, 53
Jackdaw 38
Jay 34, 47, 98, 145
Kestrel, Common 30, 31, 65, **74**, 107, 120
Kingfisher 15, 19, **20**, 118, 143, 152
Kite, Black 19, 26, 31, 106, 107
Kite, Black-shouldered 32, **86**, 106, 107, 120
Kite, Red 19, 31, 107
Knot 47, 65
Lapwing 45, 65, 80
Lark, Calandra 107
Lark, Crested **46**
Lark, Greater Short-toed **35**, 92
Lark, Lesser Short-toed 92, 115
Lark, Thekla **46**, 112
Linnet 64
Magpie 99, 106

155

Information Resources

Magpie, Azure-winged 20, 46, **58**, 64, 98, 112, 114, 141, 145
Mallard 15, 40, 106, 123
Martin, Crag 38, 46, 118, 143
Martin, House 80, 143
Martin, Sand 33, 92, 114
Moorhen 123
Nightingale 34, 106, 110, 114, 117, 118, 120, 147
Nightjar, Red-necked 15, **21**, 120, 130, 141
Nuthatch 34, 47, 92, 98, 110, 119
Oriole, Golden 15, 19, 110, 114, 141, 145
Osprey 19, 31, **33**, 38, 45, 65
Ouzel, Ring 44, 65, 106
Owl, Barn 54, 141
Owl, Eagle 54, 141
Owl, Little 15, **54**, 120
Owl, Scops 20, 54, 98, 120, 141
Owl, Tawny 54, 120, 141
Oystercatcher 15, 34
Partridge, Red-legged 106
Phalarope, Grey 54
Phalarope, Red-necked 121
Pigeon, Wood 18, 98
Pipit, Meadow 38, 44, 52, 58, 64, 69, 70, 73
Pipit, Richard's 38, 65
Pipit, Tawny 25, 35, **38**
Pipit, Tree 38, 106
Pipit, Water 70
Plover, Golden **45**, 80
Plover, Grey 15, 41, **132**, 141
Plover, Kentish 15, 106, 127, 141, **142**, 146
Plover, Little Ringed 92, 106, **118**, 143
Plover, Ringed 15
Plover, Sociable 65
Pochard, Common 40, 80
Pochard, Red-crested 15, 80, 123, **159**

Pratincole, Collared 15, **110**, 147
Quail 39, 80, 99
Raven 38, 112
Redshank, Common 15, 59, 110, 120, 127, 141, 147
Redshank, Spotted 47, 59, 75, **110**
Redstart, Black 44, 58, 64, **69**, 73
Redstart, Common 19, 25, 44
Redwing 23, 65, 69
Robin 34, 37, 44, 58, **64**, 69, 73, 128
Robin, Rufous-tailed Scrub **39**, 118, 131, 141, 143
Roller 19, **127**
Ruff 15, 47, 92, 115, 120
Sanderling 9, 15, **87**
Sandpiper, Common 118, 143
Sandpiper, Curlew 15, 47, 59, 110, **132**
Sandpiper, Green 15, 47, 106, 143
Sandpiper, Marsh 26, **121**
Sandpiper, Pectoral 121
Serin **47**, 64, 73
Shearwater, Balearic 21, 34
Shearwater, Cory's 21, 34
Shearwater, Great 34
Shearwater, Sooty 34
Shrike, Southern Grey 44, 112, **114**
Shrike, Woodchat **18**, 19, 99, 112, 141, 144
Siskin 58, 64, 65, 80
Skua, Arctic 21, 34, 47
Skua, Great **34**, 47
Skua, Pomarine 34
Skylark 37, 52, 73
Snipe, Common 41
Snipe, Jack 80
Sparrow, Rock 73
Sparrow, Spanish 45, 58, 64, 73

Sparrow, Tree 73
Sparrowhawk 31, 38, 45
Spoonbill 15, **32**, 33, 40, 53, 92, 115, 141
Starling, Common 38
Starling, Rose-coloured **38**
Starling, Spotless 20, 37, 38, 46, 53, 73, 112, 141
Stilt, Black-winged 15, 19, 26, 33, 110, **111**, 127, 141, 146
Stint, Little 15, 40
Stint, Temminck's 40, 70
Stonechat 19, 25, **37**, 44, 112
Stone-curlew 15, 40, 53, 59, **80**, 99, 120, 147
Stork, Black 32, 38, 45
Stork, White 15, 19, 33, 40, 53, **86**, **99**, 141
Storm-petrel, European 34
Storm-petrel, Wilson's 34
Swallow, Barn 52, 70, 80, 92
Swallow, Red-rumped 118, 137, 143
Swift, Chimney 38
Swift, Common 106
Swift, Pallid 15, 106
Swift, White-rumped **137**, 143
Teal 26, 75, 92
Tern, Black 15, 34, 40, 115, 120, 147
Tern, Caspian 33, 40, 59, **60**, 65
Tern, Common 34, **40**, 106
Tern, Gull-billed 106, 131
Tern, Little 15, 21, **59**, **115**, 127, 131, 141, 146
Tern, Sandwich 15, 34, 115
Thrush, Blue Rock 32, 46, 64, 98, 114, 119
Thrush, Mistle 44
Thrush, Song 44, 64, 69, **73**
Tit, Blue 20, 34, 47, 98
Tit, Crested 20, 34, 47, 98, 119, 141
Tit, Great 99

156

Red-crested Pochard

Picture Credits

The pictures in this book are the property of the copyright owners, as detailed below.

Ray Tipper: Front Cover top, Front Cover bottom far left, Front Cover bottom centre right, 4, 12, 13, 14 top, 14 bottom, 16 top, 16 bottom, 17, 18, 19, 20, 21 top, 21 bottom, 23, 24, 25 top, 25 bottom, 26, 31, 32, 33, 34, 35 top, 35 bottom, 36 top, 37, 38 top, 38 bottom, 39, 40 top, 40 bottom, 41, 42, 44 bottom, 45 top, 45 bottom, 46, 47 top, 47 bottom, 52 bottom, 53 top, 53 bottom, 54 top, 54 bottom, 57 top, 58 top, 58 bottom, 59 top, 59 bottom, 60 top, 60 bottom, 64 top, 64 bottom, 65, 69 top,73 bottom, 74, 75, 76, 77 bottom, 80, 81 bottom, 83, 85 bottom, 86 top, 86 bottom, 87 bottom, 88, 92, 93, 95 top left, 99 top 99 bottom, 100 top, 101 top, 102, 106 top, 106 bottom, 110 top, 110 bottom, 111, 112 bottom, 114 top, 114 bottom, 115, 116 bottom, 118 top, 118 bottom, 119 top, 119 bottom, 120, 121, 122 top, 122 bottom, 123, 124 top, 125 bottom, 127, 128 bottom, 129, 131 top, 131 bottom, 132 top, 132 bottom, 134 bottom, 137 top, 137 bottom, 138 top, 138 bottom, 141 top, 141 bottom, 142 top, 143, 144 top, 144 bottom, 145 bottom, 147 top, 147 bottom, 152, 159, 160, 161, Back Cover bottom far left.

Clive Viney: 22, 27, 36 bottom, 62, 63 bottom right, 81 top, 87 top, 101 bottom, 116 top, 146 top, 146 bottom, 154.

Rob Petley-Jones: 11, 52 top left, 67 top, 72, 91 bottom, 105 bottom, 107, 148.

First Nature: Front Cover bottom centre left; Front Cover bottom far right, 5, 6, 7, 8, 10, 28, 29, 30, 43, 44 top, 48, 49, 50 top, 50 bottom, 51, 52 top right, 55, 56 top, 56 bottom, 57 bottom, 61, 63 top, 63 bottom left, 66, 67 bottom, 68, 69 bottom, 70, 71, 73 top, 77 top, 78 top, 78 bottom, 79 top, 79 bottom left, 79 bottom right, 82, 84 top, 84 bottom, 85 top, 89 top, 89 bottom, 90 top, 90 bottom, 91 top, 94, 95 top right, 95 bottom, 96, 97 top, 97 bottom, 98, 100 bottom, 103 top, 103 bottom, 104, 105 top, 108, 109 top left, 109 top right, 109 bottom, 112 top, 113, 117, 124 bottom, 125 top, 126, 128 top left, 128 top right, 130, 133 top, 133 bottom, 134 top, 135, 136 top, 136 bottom, 139, 140, 142 bottom left, 145 top, Back Cover top, Back Cover bottom centre left, Back Cover bottom centre right, Back Cover bottom far right.

Pomegranate blossom

Cattle Egret

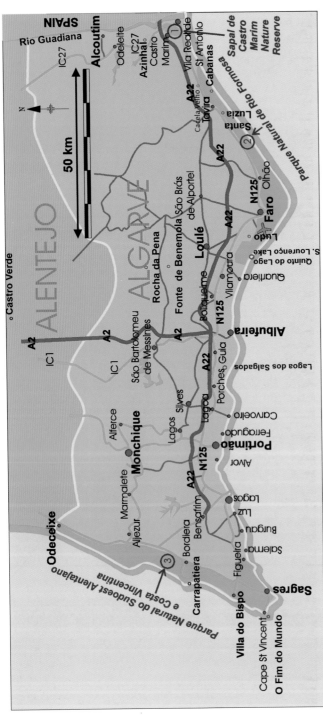

Locations cited in text